THE COMMON GRILL COOKBOOK

THE
COMMON GRILL

COOKBOOK

CHEF CRAIG COMMON

Sleeping Bear Press

Sleeping Bear Press
310 North Main Street
P.O. Box 20
Chelsea, MI 48118
www.sleepingbearpress.com

Printed and bound in Canada.

10 9 8 7 6 5 4 3

Library of Congress Cataloging-in-Publication Data

Common, Craig.
 The Common Grill Cookbook / Craig Common.
   p. cm.
 ISBN 1-886947-88-0
 1. Cookery. I. Title.
 TX714 .C636 2000
 641.57'6—dc21
              00-010784

DEDICATION

To my father, who missed seeing my dream, but I know he's here in spirit.

ACKNOWLEDGMENTS

I am grateful to:

My family; Donna, Rachel, and Brett for their support;

Chef Larry Pagliara for inspiration and for believing in me during my early years; Bob Daniels for helping make my dream come true;
my restaurant managers, present and past, for working hard toward a mutual goal; Patti and Darryl for being crazy enough to come on board at the beginning;
The entire Common Grill staff for believing in us and working so hard to make our guests happy;
Jennifer Lundahl, for providing a keen eye during the food photography and for a great layout and design;
Mark Thomas, Bob Hazen, and Carol Glover for providing great photographs of the food;
Justin, Jason, Kathy, Kate, and Anita for assisting during the photo shoots.

I am especially grateful to my mother from whom I inherited my love of food

BLACK BEAN SOUP

Basics

Sauces

Appetizers

Soups

Salads & Salad Dressings

Brunch

Meat & Poultry

Pastas & Pizza

Seafood

Vegetables & Side Dishes

Desserts

PORK TENDERLOIN WITH DRIED CHERRY COMPOTE

Preface

When it was time to join the work force at fourteen years of age, I knew that I wanted to work in a restaurant. Frank and Pat Arney hired me as a dishwasher at their restaurant, the Boar's Head Inn. From my very first day at the Inn, I knew that a restaurant was where I would hang my hat. The energy that Frank and Pat created was enormous, and even though I was only washing the dishes, I felt great going to work. I remember telling my fellow employees that one day my restaurant would be called "Common's Castle," and they all smiled and laughed.

After working for years within the Chuck Muer Organization, my dream came true on July 26, 1991 — The Common Grill opened its doors for the first time. The experience was nerve-wracking yet exciting at the same time, and I was a little overwhelmed when the first meal went out to the first guest. While it seems like only yesterday, we are quickly approaching our 10-year anniversary.

Over the years, our employees — many of them are still with us today — made my work so much easier. They have always been ready, willing, and able to embrace our policy of great hospitality that we regard with such respect and talk about nearly every day.

The Common Grill never would have happened had I not had the good fortune of meeting Bob Daniels. Bob was a longtime resident of Chelsea and had been put in charge of recruiting a restaurant for the downtown area. We had many initial discussions about the type of community Chelsea had become and what type of restaurant would best serve the needs of its residents. Bob believed in me, and in my work. And the rest, as they say, is history.

I am thrilled to be a part of the restaurant industry. For me there is nothing more satisfying than making people happy by feeding them. For that reason, it is my sincere pleasure to share my favorite recipes and my philosophies about the preparation and presentation of food with you.

Enjoy, and have fun in the kitchen!

The Common Grill

Our philosophy at The Common Grill, without question or exception, has always been to care for and meet the needs of each of our guests.

When we initially established the service philosophy, we agreed that it was not only important to treat our guests with courtesy, but to treat each other with the same kindness. The service standard that a guest should expect is defined by our teamwork. The atmosphere at The Common Grill can be defined in many ways, but we have always felt that the best thing we can offer, other than delicious food, is a genuine attitude that reflects our commitment to our guests. Our goal is to greet all of our guests with warmth and make them feel at home.

Since we opened in 1991, restaurants have evolved more than ever from serving great food to providing an overall dining experience. My goal from the beginning was to provide a great experience for everyone who came in the door, no matter what the circumstances. I felt that it was important for our guests to feel that they could come in for a pizza and salad one night, and a great fish entrée the next, without feeling that they had to dress up or dress down. Our goal is for each guest to walk out pleased that they spent some time with us.

There are many nights I wonder how we accomplish what we do, yet we continue to do it again and again. We are fortunate to have a staff that takes great pride in what they do. Many of our employees have long service records with us, and our guests have come to recognize them.

In 1993, I had the pleasure of meeting Danny Meyer at the Aspen Food and Wine Fest. Danny was the owner of Union Square Café and Gramercy Tavern in New York City, and he was in Aspen to speak about service, hospitality, and food. His restaurant had just been awarded "Best Service in America" by the James Beard Award Committee, and he was very proud. Since then his restaurants have continued to receive awards, each fully deserved. Many of the things he talked about regarding service had a great impact on me. After hearing him speak, I knew that our philosophy of hospitality was on the right track at The Common Grill.

I have always tried to keep food simple, but flavorful. It's what our kitchen is all about. During our first year of business, my friend Joe Ruicci attended the annual Chef's Dinner at Pete Peterson's restaurant, Tapawingo, in northern Michigan. Joe had the pleasure of meeting one of the featured chefs, Bradley Ogden, who was also autographing his first cookbook for the event. Joe was kind enough to ask Chef Ogden to autograph a copy for me. The inscription, "Craig, Good luck with your culinary adventures. Remember to keep it fresh, simple and fun," became my philosophy. (Although, on those crazy nights when the chefs are working as quick as lightning, when the pots and pans are clanging, when the fire at the sauté station is climbing higher and higher, when the servers are darting back and forth, when the noise and excitement are at a fever pitch and the plates are stacked up waiting to be garnished, I'm sure the staff wonders, "This is simple?!!")

Over the years, we have been blessed by the relationships that we have had with our food purveyors. They keep me aware of what is fresh and new in the market on a daily basis. We also communicate frequently about all of the foods expected at the market in the near future so I can plan my menus. It makes my job that much easier.

The energy created every night is what really makes the restaurant happen. People love to sit at the bar while they eat so they can watch the staff in the open kitchen. They marvel at the pace and the quantity of the food that is being prepared and often comment that as busy as it is back there, everything is still always served quickly, hot, and delicious.

Several years ago, on a bustling Saturday night, Bo Schembechler, former Head Coach for the University of Michigan football team, was dining at The Common Grill with his wife Kathy. I stopped by the table to greet them and exchange small talk. Bo looked around the room and commented on how busy it was and that somehow order was kept amidst the chaos.

"You know," the coach said, with that legendary gleam in his eyes, "THIS is the greatest job of coaching I have ever seen."

Basics

MASTER THE BASICS AND YOU'LL BE ON YOUR WAY TO PREPARING
THE FABULOUS FOODS FROM THIS COOKBOOK. MANY OF THE BASIC
RECIPES AND TECHNIQUES ARE THE KEY TO MAKING THE DISH
EXACTLY AS WE DO AT THE COMMON GRILL. BEGIN HERE AND I
PROMISE, THE REST IS EASY! THE QUANTITIES ARE INDICATED FOR
EACH RECIPE IN BASICS. YOU CAN CUT THEM DOWN AS NEEDED FOR
OTHER RECIPES IN THIS BOOK.

Olive Oil, Garlic, & Herb Sauce

2½ cups olive oil
6   cloves garlic, roasted (see page 25)
3   tablespoons seafood base (see page 202)
1   cup hot water
2   tablespoons parsley, finely chopped
2   sun dried tomatoes, finely chopped

Place 1 cup of olive oil in food processor with garlic. Process until garlic is thoroughly blended. Set aside.

In small bowl mix seafood base with ½ cup of hot water. Stir until completely dissolved. Set aside.

Place remaining olive oil in saucepan and heat until just below boiling.

Add garlic and oil mixture and immediately remove from heat, stir to mix well. Stir in parsley and sun dried tomatoes. Add seafood base mixture and remaining ½ cup hot water. Whisk entire mixture until thoroughly combined. Refrigerate.

Makes 3½ cups

Tomato-Basil Sauce

2   tablespoons olive oil
2   cloves garlic, finely chopped
1   small onion, finely chopped
2   teaspoons fresh basil, finely chopped
2   teaspoons fresh oregano, finely chopped
1   tablespoon parsley, finely chopped
¼   cup dry chardonnay wine
1   28 oz. can Italian plum tomatoes, chopped
1   tablespoon seafood base (see page 202)

Heat olive oil in large saucepan. Do not boil. Add garlic and onions. Sauté until soft. Stir in herbs and cook for 1 minute. Add wine, tomatoes, and seafood base. Mix well. Bring to a boil and continue cooking for 10 minutes.

Store in refrigerator.

Makes 4 cups

Parmesan Cream

1   cup heavy cream
1   egg yolk, lightly beaten
2   tablespoons Olive Oil, Garlic, & Herb Sauce (see page 18)
1   tablespoon freshly grated Parmesan cheese

In a small bowl, thoroughly mix together cream and egg yolk. Refrigerate until ready to use.

Heat Olive Oil, Garlic, & Herb Sauce in a sauté pan. Add cream and egg mixture, stirring until slightly thickened. Stir in Parmesan cheese and continue cooking until cheese is completely blended in cream mixture.

Makes 1 cup

Garlic Butter

1   cup butter, softened
1   clove garlic, roasted (see page 25)
¼   cup dry white wine
2   teaspoons parsley, finely chopped
1   tablespoon roasted yellow pepper, diced (see page 25)
1   tablespoon roasted red pepper, diced (see page 25)
½   teaspoon kosher salt
¼   teaspoon cracked black pepper

Beat softened butter at medium speed with mixer until soft and fluffy. Set aside.

In food processor, blend garlic, wine and parsley until thoroughly mixed. Add remaining ingredients and butter; mix well. Refrigerate.

Makes 1 cup

Tomato Concasse

1   cup plum tomatoes, seeded & diced into small pieces
2   tablespoons extra virgin olive oil
1   teaspoon black pepper
2   teaspoons kosher salt
1½   teaspoons chives, chopped

Thoroughly mix all ingredients. Refrigerate until ready to use.

Makes 1 cup

Roasted Tomato Sauce

1   lb. plum tomatoes, halved
2   tablespoons shallots, chopped
3   cloves garlic
½   cup olive oil
¼   teaspoon black pepper
1   sprig fresh thyme
1   sprig fresh chives
1   sprig fresh oregano
2   tablespoons balsamic vinegar
½   teaspoon salt

Preheat oven to 450°.

Place tomatoes in heavy baking pan with shallots and garlic. Drizzle with olive oil. Sprinkle with black pepper and herbs. Bake in oven for 30 minutes, or until tomatoes are well done.

Remove from oven and place ingredients in food processor. Purée until well blended. Add vinegar and salt and purée again.

Refrigerate until ready to use.

Makes 4 cups

Basil Pesto

4	cloves garlic
1	teaspoon salt
½	lb. basil leaves
¼	cup pine nuts
1	cup olive oil
½	cup Parmesan cheese, freshly grated
2	teaspoons Romano cheese, freshly grated
¼	cup butter, softened

Place garlic, salt, basil, pine nuts, and olive oil in the bowl of a food processor, fitted with the metal blade, and process until mixture is smooth. Add cheeses and butter and process again until mixture is smooth.

Store in refrigerator.

Makes 2 cups

Fresh Tomato Salsa

6	plum tomatoes, seeded and chopped into small pieces
2	teaspoons cilantro, finely chopped
1	jalapeño pepper, seeded and finely chopped
½	small red onion, finely chopped
1	clove garlic, finely chopped
1	teaspoon fresh lime juice
½	teaspoon salt
¼	teaspoon ground black pepper

Place all ingredients in a medium bowl; mix well. Refrigerate.

Makes 1 cup

Tomato Butter Sauce

⅓ cup olive oil
1 small carrot, sliced thin
¼ cup leeks, sliced thin
3 cups Tomato-Basil Sauce (see page 18)
⅔ cup Chicken Stock (see page 23)
¼ teaspoon cayenne pepper
½ lb. butter, cut into small pieces
2 teaspoons chives

Heat olive oil in large sauté pan. Sauté carrot and leeks until soft. Stir in Tomato-Basil Sauce and mix well. Cook for 5 minutes. Add Chicken Stock and cayenne pepper; cook over high heat until the liquid is evaporated and the sauce is thick, approximately 15 to 20 minutes.

Carefully pour sauce mixture into food processor and blend until smooth.

Return to pan and gradually whisk in butter until well blended. Add chopped chives. Refrigerate until ready to use.

Makes 4 cups

Red Bell Pepper Butter

1 lb. butter, softened
2 red bell peppers, roasted, seeded, skins removed (see page 25)
2 tablespoons butter, melted
4 cloves garlic
1 green onion, coarsely chopped
1 teaspoon parsley, finely chopped
½ teaspoon cayenne pepper
½ teaspoon fresh thyme, finely chopped

Place softened butter in bowl and beat until very fluffy. Set aside.

Place red peppers, melted butter, garlic, and onion in food processor. Purée.

Transfer to softened butter mixture; add chopped parsley, cayenne pepper, and thyme and mix thoroughly.

Refrigerate until ready to use.

Makes 1 lb.

Chicken Stock

1	gallon water
5	lbs. chicken bones
1	onion, diced
2	ribs celery, diced
2	carrots, diced
1	leek, thoroughly cleaned & diced
1	tablespoon kosher salt
2	cloves garlic, diced
1	tablespoon cracked black pepper
4	sprigs fresh basil
4	sprigs fresh parsley
4	sprigs fresh thyme

Place all ingredients in a large stockpot. Cover and bring to a boil. Reduce heat and simmer for 2 hours. Remove chicken bones and strain.

Refrigerate until ready to use.

Makes 2 quarts

Brown Chicken Stock

2½	lbs. chicken bones
4	tablespoons olive oil
2	red onions, sliced thin
1	rib celery, chopped
2	carrots, diced
8	cups water
1	head of garlic, cut in half
1	sprig fresh thyme
1	sprig fresh parsley
1	sprig fresh basil
2	teaspoons kosher salt
1	teaspoon cracked black pepper

Preheat oven to 450°.

Roast chicken bones in oven for 1 hour, or until browned. After 30 minutes remove from oven and discard any fat. Return to oven for remaining 30 minutes.

Heat olive oil in stockpot over medium heat. Add onions, celery and carrots and cook until golden. Reduce heat and continue cooking for an additional 10 minutes, or until well browned.

Transfer chicken bones to stockpot and add enough water to cover bones by 2″. Bring to a boil. Stir in garlic, thyme, parsley, basil, salt & pepper. Reduce heat to low and simmer for 2 hours. Add water as needed.

Strain. Transfer liquid to a clean stockpot. Simmer over low heat for an additional hour. Remove from heat and strain again.

Refrigerate until ready to use.

Makes 1 quart

Fish Stock

2½ lbs. fish bones
1   small yellow onion, sliced thin
8   sprigs fresh parsley
2   sprigs fresh thyme
1   sprig fresh basil
4   cups water
1   cup white wine

Place all ingredients in a stockpot and bring to a slow boil. Reduce heat and simmer for 30 minutes. Remove from heat and allow to rest for 15 minutes. Strain.

Refrigerate until ready to use.

Makes 1 quart

Beef Stock

5   lbs. beef bones
2   tablespoons olive oil
¼   cup tomato paste
1   cup Spanish onion, chopped
½   cup carrots, chopped
½   cup celery, chopped
1   head garlic, halved
1   gallon cold water
2   sprigs thyme
2   sprigs oregano
2   sprigs parsley
4   sprigs basil
2   teaspoons kosher salt

Preheat oven to 450°.

Place beef bones in an ovenproof pan. Drizzle olive oil over bones. Bake in oven for 30 minutes, or until bones are brown.

Transfer bones to a stockpot. Add tomato paste, onions, carrots, celery, garlic, thyme, oregano, parsley, basil, and salt. Pour in water and bring to a boil. When water boils, reduce heat and simmer for 2 hours. Remove from heat and strain.

Refrigerate until ready to use.

Makes 2 quarts

Roasted Garlic

2 heads garlic, cut in half
2 tablespoons olive oil
1 teaspoon kosher salt

Preheat oven to 400˚.

In a small bowl, toss garlic, olive oil, and salt together. Place in oven-proof baking dish and bake for 15 to 20 minutes, or until golden. Remove from oven and allow to cool.

Squeeze the garlic from each of the heads.

Roasted Peppers

Wash peppers and dry thoroughly.

Grilling
Place peppers on grill and heat on all sides until the skins are black and blistered.

Broiling
Place peppers on a broiler pan and position rack so that peppers are 6˝ from the flame. Broil on all sides until skins are black and blistered.

Once peppers are black and blistered, immediately remove from heat and place in a bowl. Cover with plastic wrap and allow to cool.

Peel off the skin and cut peppers in half. Remove the seeds and membrane.

Smoked Chicken

6 chicken breasts (see page 202)
2 cups water
2 tablespoons sugar
2 tablespoons brown sugar
2 tablespoons kosher salt
1 bay leaf
4 juniper berries, crushed
2 sprigs thyme
1 teaspoon Worcestershire sauce
4 garlic cloves

Trim excess fat from chicken.

Mix all remaining ingredients together in a bowl. Place chicken in bowl and marinate for 24 hours in refrigerator.

Preheat grill.

Rinse chicken under cold water.

Fill the bottom of a 9x13″ stainless steel pan with water-soaked wood chips. Place a wire rack over wood chips. Arrange chicken on rack and cover tightly with aluminum foil.

Place pan on grill and smoke for 30 to 40 minutes. Remove chicken and place in clean pan.

Preheat oven to 350°.

Bake chicken in oven for 20 to 30 minutes, or until completely cooked. Cool.

Polenta

1 cup water
1 cup chicken stock
1 teaspoon garlic, minced
½ cup yellow cornmeal
⅓ cup sour cream
¼ cup Monterey Jack cheese, shredded
¼ cup Parmesan cheese, shredded
2 tablespoons butter
¼ teaspoon salt
⅛ teaspoon white pepper

Preheat oven to 350°.

In a medium ovenproof saucepan bring water, chicken stock, and garlic to a boil, stir in cornmeal, reduce heat and cook for 5 minutes, stirring constantly.

Cover pan and place in oven. Bake for 30 minutes.

Remove from oven and stir in sour cream, cheeses, butter, salt, and pepper. Pour into a greased 11x13″ baking dish, cool and allow to set.

Cut into 2x2″ squares, circles, or any shape you desire.

Sauces

IN ADDITION TO THE SAUCES IN THE BASICS CHAPTER, THESE SAUCES WILL ENHANCE OTHER RECIPES THAT YOU MIGHT HAVE SEEN ELSEWHERE.

Basil Aioli

1	egg yolk
1	garlic clove, finely chopped
¼	teaspoon lemon juice
¼	teaspoon Dijon mustard
⅛	teaspoon cayenne pepper
¼	cup olive oil
2	tablespoons heavy cream
1½	tablespoons Basil Pesto (see page 21)

Place egg yolk, garlic, lemon juice, mustard, and cayenne pepper in a food processor and blend well.

Add olive oil slowly until blended well.

Add cream and Basil Pesto and mix very well.

Makes ½ cup

Great for sandwiches.

Sun Dried Tomato Pesto

4	tablespoons sun dried tomatoes
¼	cup olive oil
2	teaspoons pine nuts
¼	teaspoon fresh thyme
½	teaspoon garlic, finely chopped
¼	teaspoon salt
⅛	teaspoon white pepper
1	teaspoon butter
2	teaspoon Parmesan cheese, grated

In a blender combine tomatoes, olive oil, pine nuts, thyme, garlic, salt, pepper, and butter. Blend until smooth.

Add Parmesan cheese and blend.

Refrigerate until ready to use.

Makes ½ cup

Great on fish, pizza, and vegetables.

Tomato Leek Fondue

2	tablespoons butter
¼	cup extra virgin olive oil
1	leek, sliced into ¼″ pieces
2	garlic cloves, minced
4 to 6	lg. tomatoes, preferably beefsteak, peeled, seeded, and chopped
2	tablespoons tomato paste
2	teaspoons basil, finely chopped
2	tablespoons sugar
1	teaspoon black pepper

Heat butter and olive oil in large sauté pan until hot, but not boiling. Sauté leek until soft, approximately 8 to 10 minutes. Add all remaining ingredients and simmer for 30 minutes. Remove from heat.

Makes 1 qt.

This sauce is an excellent accompaniment for whitefish.

Citrus Aioli

2	garlic cloves
2	teaspoons lime zest
2	teaspoons orange zest
2	teaspoons lemon zest
1	tablespoon fresh lime juice
1	tablespoon fresh orange juice
1	tablespoon lemon juice
2	egg yolks
½	teaspoon paprika
½	teaspoon kosher salt
½	teaspoon black pepper
1	tablespoon water
2	teaspoons cilantro, finely chopped
2	teaspoons parsley, finely chopped
1	cup olive oil

Place all ingredients except olive oil in food processor and purée. With processor running, slowly drizzle in olive oil. Blend well. Refrigerate until ready to serve.

Makes 1½ cups

Great on any grilled fish.

Asian BBQ Honey Vinaigrette

½	cup teriyaki sauce
¼	cup honey
¼	cup rice wine vinegar
¼	cup sesame oil
1	tablespoon ginger, grated
1	green onion, thinly sliced
1	clove garlic, minced
1	teaspoon Chinese Chili Paste (see page 202)

Put all ingredients in blender and process until well blended.

Refrigerate until ready to use.

Makes 1 cup

This is also great on grilled salmon or yellowfin tuna.

Bacon-Balsamic Vinaigrette

6	oz. bacon, cut into ½″ pieces
½	cup olive oil
2	tablespoons shallots, finely chopped
2	garlic cloves, minced
1	tablespoon brown sugar
⅓	cup balsamic vinegar

Cook bacon until crispy. Drain bacon oil and reserve. Set aside.

Pour ¼ cup of bacon oil into sauté pan with olive oil. Heat. Add shallots, garlic, and brown sugar; sauté until shallots are soft, approximately 3 to 4 minutes. Stir in balsamic vinegar. Add cooked bacon and mix well. Refrigerate until ready to serve.

Makes 1 cup

This is used in a salmon recipe but would be great on a spinach salad.

Red Pepper Coulis

1	tablespoon olive oil
3	red bell peppers, roasted, peeled, and chopped (see page 25)
2	tablespoons red onions, finely chopped
1	garlic clove, minced
½	cup Chicken Stock (see page 23)
4	tablespoons red wine
¼	teaspoon salt
⅛	teaspoon black pepper
2	teaspoons chilled butter
1	teaspoon fresh basil, finely chopped

Heat olive oil in medium sauté pan. Add peppers, onions, and garlic; sauté until tender, approximately 6 to 8 minutes. Stir in Chicken Stock and red wine; continue to cook for 10 minutes on medium heat. Add salt & pepper. Purée in blender or food processor. Strain. Add chilled butter and basil; mix well.

Refrigerate until ready to use.

Makes 2 cups

Great on swordfish or halibut.

Lemon Garlic Aioli

2	garlic cloves
½	teaspoon kosher salt
2	egg yolks
2	tablespoons lemon juice
½	teaspoon cracked black pepper
⅛	teaspoon cayenne pepper
1	cup olive oil
1	tablespoon lemon zest

Place garlic and kosher salt in food processor and process until finely chopped. Add egg yolks, lemon juice, black pepper, and cayenne pepper; mix well. With machine running slowly drizzle in olive oil. Add lemon zest and process until blended.

Refrigerate until ready to use.

Makes 1½ cups

Great for calamari, smelt, or lake perch.

Raspberry Mint Sauce

4	tablespoons fresh mint, finely chopped
2	cups frozen raspberries, thawed
⅓	cup white wine vinegar
2	tablespoons raspberry vinegar
1	tablespoon fresh lemon juice
3	tablespoons super fine sugar

Place all ingredients in medium saucepan and bring to a boil. Continue boiling over medium heat until sauce is reduced by half. Place in blender and purée. Strain and allow to cool.

Heat sauce when ready to serve.

Makes 1 cup

This is great on lamb chops.

Olive Relish

¼	cup green Arnaud olives, pitted & chopped
¼	cup Calamata olives, chopped
¼	cup pitted oil cured black olives, chopped
¼	cup red bell pepper, roasted, chopped (see page 25)
1	tablespoon parsley, finely chopped
2	anchovy fillets, finely chopped
1	teaspoon capers, chopped
1	teaspoon red wine vinegar
2	garlic cloves, minced
2	tablespoons extra virgin olive oil

Combine all ingredients in medium bowl and mix well.

Refrigerate until ready to serve.

Makes 1 cup

Excellent on full flavored fish, swordfish, or sea bass.

Red Pepper - Garlic Mayonnaise

⅔ cup mayonnaise
¼ teaspoon dry mustard
⅛ teaspoon cayenne pepper
¼ cup Red Bell Pepper Butter, melted
    (see page 22)
1 tablespoon Garlic Butter, melted
    (see page 19)

In medium bowl, using wire whisk, beat together mayonnaise, dry mustard, and cayenne pepper. Add Red Bell Pepper Butter and beat until creamy. Mix in Garlic Butter.

Refrigerate until ready to use.

Makes 1 cup

Great on sandwiches.

Santa Fe Chili Butter

2 tablespoons butter, melted
1 jalapeño pepper, seeded
1 clove garlic
1 green onion
1 tablespoon Worcestershire sauce
1 teaspoon hot sauce
1 lb. butter, softened
1½ teaspoons oregano
1 tablespoon chili powder
1 teaspoon paprika
1 teaspoon red pepper flakes
½ teaspoon cumin

Place melted butter, jalapeño pepper, garlic, green onion, Worcestershire sauce, and hot sauce in food processor and blend until thoroughly mixed. Add softened butter and process until well blended. Add remaining ingredients and process until well mixed.

Refrigerate until ready to use.

Makes 1 lb.

Great on steak, chicken, and fish.

Pistachio Basil Butter

½	cup pistachios, chopped
1	tablespoon basil, chopped
½	cup butter, softened
¼	cup clarified butter
2	cloves garlic, minced
½	teaspoon salt
1	teaspoon black pepper
2	teaspoons sugar
2	tablespoons lime juice

Place all ingredients in blender or food processor and process until thoroughly mixed.

Makes 1 cup

Great on grilled fish.

Papaya, Mango, & Lime Salsa

1	papaya, peeled, seeded, diced into ½″ pieces
1	mango, peeled, diced into ½″ pieces
1	red bell pepper, roasted, peeled, seeded, diced into ¼″ pieces (see page 25)
2	tablespoons cilantro, finely chopped
¼	cup fresh lime juice
1	clove garlic, minced
½	cup olive oil
¼	teaspoon salt
⅛	teaspoon hot sauce

Combine all ingredients in medium bowl; mix well.

Refrigerate until ready to serve.

Makes 2 cups

This is fantastic on grilled salmon.

Spicy Garlic Fennel Oil

¼ cup olive oil
1 clove garlic, crushed
½ teaspoon black pepper
1 teaspoon fennel seed
2 teaspoons red pepper flakes

Combine all ingredients in a heavy saucepan. Bring to a boil. Reduce heat to low and simmer for 10 minutes. Remove from heat, set aside for 30 minutes. Strain.

Makes ¼ cup

This is used for our Asian Slaw.

Tomato & Roasted Pepper Compote

¼ cup white wine
¼ cup golden raisins
¼ cup raisins
1 red bell pepper, roasted, diced into 1˝ pieces (see page 25)
1 yellow bell pepper, roasted, diced into 1˝ pieces (see page 25)
3 plum tomatoes, seeded, cut into 1˝ pieces
⅓ cup extra virgin olive oil
1 leek, washed, sliced into ½˝ pieces
1 small zucchini, diced into 1˝ pieces
2 cloves garlic, minced
¼ cup pine nuts, toasted
¼ cup fresh basil, julienned in thin strips
2 tablespoons balsamic vinegar
1 tablespoon kosher salt
1 teaspoon black pepper

Simmer raisins and white wine over medium heat until soft, approximately 2 to 3 minutes. Set aside.

In medium bowl combine peppers and tomatoes. Set aside.

Heat 2 tablespoons of olive oil in medium sauté pan. Add leek; cook until limp, approximately 3 to 4 minutes. Add to pepper-tomato mixture.

Heat another 2 tablespoons olive oil in sauté pan. Add zucchini; cook until tender. Add to pepper-tomato mixture.

Drain raisins and combine with pepper-tomato mixture. Add remaining ingredients, including remaining olive oil; mix well. Season with kosher salt & pepper.

Refrigerate until ready to use.

Makes 2 cups

This is great on grilled fish.

Grilled Maple Corn & Bacon Relish

½	cup fresh corn kernels
3	tablespoons maple syrup
2	bacon slices, diced small
¼	cup red onions, diced small
2	tablespoons red pepper, diced small
1	teaspoons fresh thyme, chopped fine
⅛	teaspoons salt
⅛	teaspoons pepper

Brush corn with maple syrup and grill until carmelized. Remove corn off the cob.

Cook bacon until very crisp in sauté pan. Add onions and cook until translucent. Add red peppers and corn and cook for two minutes. Add thyme, salt and pepper and mix well.

Remove from stove and keep warm until ready to serve.

Makes 1 cup

This is great on pork tenderloin.

Sauces

36

Mint Aioli

3	egg yolks
4	tablespoons fresh mint, chopped
½	teaspoon garlic, chopped
⅔	cup mint oil
½	teaspoon salt
	pinch white pepper
2	tablespoons lemon juice

Mint Oil

⅔	cup olive oil
8	sprigs fresh mint

Place egg yolks, mint, and garlic in food processor or blender and process until thoroughly combined.

With machine running, add mint oil in a slow steady stream. Process until smooth.

Add salt, pepper, and lemon juice and mix well.

Mint Oil: Heat olive oil in sauté pan. Add mint, toss to coat and immediately remove from heat.

Steep for 30 minutes. Strain.

Makes 1 cup

A great addition to grilled lamb chops.

Appetizers

I HAVE ALWAYS FELT THAT STARTING A DINNER PARTY WITH GREAT
APPETIZERS SETS THE TONE OF THE DINNER. THE RECIPES IN THE
FOLLOWING PAGES REFLECT A LOT OF FUN THAT WE'VE HAD IN THE
RESTAURANT WITH DIFFERENT STYLES OF FOOD FROM ASIAN APPE-
TIZERS TO MIDWEST CATFISH TO SOUTHWEST QUESADILLAS.

20 jumbo shrimp, tails on, deveined, butterflied

cornstarch for dusting

¼ cup vegetable oil

½ cup Firecracker Sauce

½ cup pea pods, cleaned

½ cup red peppers, julienned into ¼″ strips

½ cup yellow peppers, julienned into ¼″ strips

1 tablespoon green onions, sliced into ½″ pieces

1 cup napa cabbage, julienned fine

1 cup Hong Kong Salsa

2 sprigs fresh cilantro, finely chopped

Firecracker Sauce

¼ cup tomato paste

2 tablespoons water

1 tablespoon teriyaki sauce

1 tablespoon dry chardonnay wine

1 teaspoon sugar

¼ teaspoon salt

2 tablespoons Chinese chili paste (see page 202)

2 cloves garlic, finely chopped

1 tablespoon ginger, finely chopped

1 teaspoon red pepper flakes

Hong Kong Salsa

⅔ cup fresh plum tomatoes, peeled, seeded, & diced into ¼″ pieces

2 tablespoons green onion, finely chopped

1 teaspoon fresh ginger, minced

1 tablespoon Chinese chili paste (see page 202)

1½ tablespoons red wine vinegar

1 teaspoon peanut oil

1 tablespoon sesame oil

1 tablespoon cilantro, finely chopped

½ teaspoon sugar

½ teaspoon salt

1 jalapeño pepper, finely chopped

To prepare shrimp: Lightly dust shrimp in cornstarch. Heat vegetable oil in a large sauté pan. Add shrimp; cook for approximately 1 minute or until shrimp are golden in color.

Add Firecracker Sauce, stir to coat shrimp.

Add pea pods, red & yellow peppers, and green onions; sauté until tender; 2 to 3 minutes.

Line each serving plate with ¼ cup napa cabbage. Spoon sautéed vegetables over the cabbage. Gently place 5 shrimp on each plate, evenly distribute the sautéed vegetables over top of shrimp. Sprinkle with chopped cilantro.

Serve with Hong Kong Salsa for dipping.

Firecracker Sauce: Combine all ingredients in medium bowl and mix thoroughly. Refrigerate until ready to use.

Hong Kong Salsa: Combine all ingredients in a medium size bowl. Mix well. Cover and refrigerate until ready to use.

Bonny Doon Cardinal Zinfandel

Stuffed Blue Corn Chile Peppers with Roasted Tomato-Ancho Sauce, Tomato Salsa, and Chipotle Cream Sauce

8	large Poblano chile peppers
16	oz. cheese mix
	all-purpose flour for dusting
4	eggs, beaten
	blue corn flour mix for dusting
½	cup olive oil
	Roasted Tomato-Ancho Sauce
	Fresh Tomato Salsa
	Chipotle Cream
8	teaspoons parsley, chopped, for garnish

Cheese Mix

1	cup Monterey Jack cheese, shredded
⅔	cup goat cheese, shredded
⅓	cup jalapeño jack cheese or Rustico Red Pepper cheese*, shredded

Blue Corn Flour Mix

½	cup blue cornmeal
2	teaspoons ground cumin
2	teaspoons black pepper
2	teaspoons kosher salt
1	teaspoon oregano
	pinch cayenne pepper

Roasted Tomato-Ancho Sauce

12	plum tomatoes, halved
1	large red onion, quartered
6	cloves garlic, roasted (see page 25)
2	tablespoons olive oil, for roasting

To prepare Blue Corn Chile Peppers: Broil peppers on high heat until skins begin to blister. Remove from heat, place in plastic bag, and cool. Once cool, peel skins, slit pepper lengthwise on one side and carefully remove seeds. Fill each pepper with ¼ cup of the Cheese Mix and close, overlapping ends to prevent cheese mixture from spilling out of pepper.

Roll peppers first in all-purpose flour, then dip in beaten egg and roll once again, this time in the blue corn flour. Place on a cookie sheet, lined with waxed paper, and refrigerate until ready to use.

Sauté peppers in olive oil until golden on all sides, approximately 5 minutes.

Return peppers to lined cookie sheet and bake in 400° oven for 6-8 minutes, or until cheese begins to melt.

To serve: Ladle hot Tomato-Ancho Sauce onto serving platter. Place peppers in center of sauce, spoon Tomato Salsa over peppers and drizzle with Chipotle Cream. Garnish with chopped parsley.

Cheese Mix: Mix all ingredients well. Refrigerate.

Blue Corn Flour Mix: Mix all ingredients until well blended.

Roasted Tomato-Ancho Sauce: Preheat oven to 450°.

Brush tomatoes and onions with olive oil and roast in oven for 30 minutes. Turn oven to broiler setting and blister the skins. Remove from broiler, transfer mixture to food processor and purée for 5 seconds. Add remaining ingredients and blend well. Refrigerate until ready to use.

Fresh Tomato Salsa: Place all ingredients in medium bowl. Mix well. Refrigerate.

Chipotle Cream Sauce: Place all ingredients in food processor and process until well blended. Refrigerate until ready to use.

Serve with margaritas.

⅓   cup fresh lime juice

2   chipotle peppers, canned in adobo
    sauce

½   teaspoon ancho chile powder

½   teaspoon ground cumin

2   tablespoons extra virgin olive oil

Fresh Tomato Salsa

3   plum tomatoes, seeded & chopped
    into small pieces

½   teaspoon cilantro, finely chopped

½   jalapeño pepper, seeded & finely
    chopped

¼   small red onion, finely chopped

½   clove garlic, finely chopped
    squeeze of fresh lime juice

¼   teaspoon salt
    pinch ground black pepper

Chipotle Cream Sauce

1   tablespoon sour cream

1   tablespoon goat cheese

½   teaspoon canned chipotle pepper in
    adobo sauce

1   teaspoon cilantro

¼   cup heavy cream

** Rustico Red Pepper Cheese is an Italian semi-hard cheese
with red pepper flakes. It is available through specialty
stores—please refer to page 202 for more information.*

Prepare the Cheese Mix, Roasted Tomato-Ancho Sauce, Salsa, and Chipotle Cream Sauce the day before and refrigerate. Makes final preparations a snap!

New Bedford Littleneck Clams

32 littleneck clams in shells, washed well

4 oz. Italian sausage, casing removed, chopped

4 teaspoons jalapeño pepper, seeded & finely chopped

½ small red onion, sliced thin

pinch red pepper flakes

1 cup Garlic Butter

1 cup water

1 cup Tomato-Basil Sauce (see page 18)

1 cup dry chardonnay wine

4 green onions, sliced thin

4 pieces garlic bread

Garlic Butter

1 cup butter, softened

1 clove garlic, roasted (see page 25)

¼ cup dry white wine

2 teaspoons parsley, finely chopped

1 tablespoon roasted yellow pepper, diced (see page 25)

1 tablespoon roasted red pepper, diced (see page 25)

½ teaspoon kosher salt

¼ teaspoon cracked black pepper

Place clams, sausage, pepper, onion, red pepper flakes, Garlic Butter, water, Tomato-Basil Sauce and wine in saucepan and cook on medium heat until all clams are open, approximately 5 to 6 minutes.

Distribute clams evenly in serving bowl and pour sauce over top of clams. Top with green onions and serve with grilled garlic bread.

Garlic Butter: Beat softened butter at medium speed with mixer until soft and fluffy. Set aside.

In food processor, blend garlic and wine until thoroughly mixed. Transfer mixture to a bowl; add remaining ingredients and softened butter; mix well. Refrigerate.

Appetizers

42

Frog's Leap Zinfandel - Napa | *As an entrée, this dish will serve 2 people.*

Grilled Herb Bread with Baked Brie Cheese

Herb Pizza Dough, page 141

4   4 oz. pieces domestic Brie cheese
4   teaspoons butter
    Spicy Apple Chutney
4   teaspoons chives, chopped
4   teaspoons toasted almonds

Spicy Apple Chutney
1   tablespoon vegetable oil
¼   very small red onion, diced fine
¼   red bell pepper, diced fine
¼   teaspoon dry mustard
     pinch salt
1   clove garlic, minced
½   jalapeño pepper, minced
3   Granny Smith apples, peeled, core
        removed, diced into ½″ pieces
     pinch ground allspice
     pinch ground ginger
1   tablespoon golden raisins
3   tablespoons brown sugar
2   tablespoons red wine vinegar

Prepare Herb Pizza Dough. Set aside.

Preheat oven to 400°.

Arrange Brie in ovenproof pan. Dot with butter. Bake in oven until cheese begins to puff, approximately 8 minutes.

Transfer Brie to serving plate, spoon warm Spicy Apple Chutney around Brie. Top with chives and toasted almonds.

Brush herb bread with olive oil. Grill on both sides, making sure to get grill marks on bread. Cut in quarters. Arrange bread around cheese.

Spicy Apple Chutney: Heat vegetable oil in sauté pan. Add red onion, red pepper, mustard, and salt; cook until translucent, approximately 5 minutes. Add garlic, jalapeño pepper, apples, allspice, and ginger; continue cooking for one minute. Add raisins, brown sugar, and vinegar and bring to a boil. Refrigerate until ready to use.

Appetizers

43

Bernardus Chardonnay – Monterey County

16 pieces spring roll wrapper
Spicy Asian Slaw
Chinese Mustard Sauce
8 teaspoons Spicy Garlic Fennel Oil
(see page 35)
4 teaspoons chives, chopped
½ cup vegetable oil

Lobster Mixture

1 teaspoon curry powder
1 tablespoon unsweetened coconut milk
1 tablespoon soy sauce
1 tablespoon cider vinegar
1 lb. lobster meat, precooked, cut
in ½″ pieces

Spring Roll Filling

2 oz. rice-stick noodles
2 tablespoons peanut oil
2 teaspoons garlic, minced
1 tablespoon ginger, grated
1 jalapeño pepper, seeded, chopped fine
½ cup carrots, julienned, fine
½ cup red bell peppers, julienned fine
¼ cup pea pods, julienned fine
¼ cup green onions, sliced on bias
2 cups napa cabbage, cut into 1″ pieces
1 teaspoon curry powder
¼ teaspoon kosher salt
¼ teaspoon sugar
2 teaspoons soy sauce
1 tablespoon cider vinegar
1 tablespoon cilantro, chopped fine
2 eggs, beaten, to seal spring rolls

Lobster Mixture: Combine curry powder, coconut milk, soy sauce, and cider vinegar in medium bowl and mix well. Add lobster and marinate for 1 hour.

Spring Rolls Preparation: Blanch rice-stick noodles in warm water until soft, approximately 5 minutes. Drain and cut into 2″ pieces. Set aside.

Heat peanut oil in large sauté pan. Add garlic, ginger, and jalapeño peppers and cook for 1 to 2 minutes. Add carrots, red peppers, pea pods and green onions and cook for 2 to 3 minutes. Add napa cabbage and cook for another three minutes. Add curry powder, salt, sugar, soy sauce, and cider vinegar and cook for 3 to 4 minutes longer. Add rice-stick noodles and chopped cilantro; mix well. Add Chicken Stock Roux and mix well. Remove from heat; cool. Fold in lobster and mix well.

Place ¼ cup of filling in each spring roll wrapper. Wrap tightly and seal with beaten egg. Refrigerate until ready to use.

Heat vegetable oil in large sauté pan. Sauté spring rolls on both sides until golden and crispy, approximately 5 minutes.

To serve: Spoon Asian Slaw onto platter. Cut spring rolls in half on the bias and arrange on the Asian Slaw. Drizzle with warm Spicy Garlic Fennel Oil, followed by Chinese Mustard Sauce. Garnish with chopped chives.

Spicy Asian Slaw: In small bowl combine lime juice, red onion, soy sauce, ginger, jalapeño pepper, garlic, honey, curry powder, sesame oil and peanut oil, mix well. Set aside.

In a separate medium size bowl, combine napa cabbage, carrots, red and yellow peppers, green onions, cilantro, and toasted sesame seeds with salt and pepper. Toss. Add lime juice mixture; toss to coat.

Chinese Mustard Sauce: Mix together and refrigerate. (Makes ½ cup.)

Murphy-Goode Fume Blanc - Napa

Chicken Stock Roux

1   tablespoon chicken stock
1   tablespoon cornstarch

Spicy Asian Slaw

2   teaspoons lime juice
¼   cup red onion, finely chopped
¼   teaspoon soy sauce
½   teaspoon ginger, grated
¼   teaspoon jalapeño pepper
½   teaspoon garlic, minced
¼   teaspoon honey
    pinch curry powder
¼   teaspoon sesame oil
1   tablespoon peanut oil
½   cup napa cabbage, sliced thin
1   tablespoon carrots, sliced thin
1   tablespoon red bell pepper, julienned
        into thin pieces
1   tablespoon yellow pepper, julienned
        into thin pieces
2   teaspoons green onions, chopped
2   teaspoons cilantro, finely chopped
½   teaspoon sesame seeds, toasted
¼   teaspoon kosher salt
    pinch black pepper

Chinese Mustard Sauce

2   tablespoons dry mustard
2   tablespoons red wine vinegar
2   teaspoons mayonnaise
2   tablespoons Hoisin sauce (see page
        202)

You could use shrimp, chicken or increase spring roll filling for vegetable spring rolls.

Skillet Roasted Mussels

60 mussels, cleaned and debearded
1 cup Garlic Butter, (see page 19)
1 cup cooking sherry
1 cup + 4 tablespoon Tomato
    Concasse (see page 20)
1 cup water
4 teaspoons chopped chives
4 pieces garlic bread, grilled

Preheat oven to 400°.

In large ovenproof pan, combine mussels, Garlic Butter, sherry, water, and 1 cup of Tomato Concasse. Bake in oven until mussels are opened, approximately 10-15 minutes.

Ladle into serving bowls. Top with chives and remaining Tomato Concasse. Serve with garlic bread.

Chateau St. Jean Fume Blanc - Sonoma County

24 sea scallops, medium size
flour for dusting
4 tablespoons olive oil
4 Smoked Salmon Cakes
Cucumber-Thyme Salad
4 tablespoons Roasted Lemon
Vinaigrette
4 teaspoons parsley, chopped for
garnish

Smoked Salmon Cakes
½ cup peppered smoked salmon
½ cup Potato Leek Cake Mix
2 tablespoons butter, melted

Potato Leek Cake Mix
1 large baking potato
pinch salt
pinch black pepper
1 egg, lightly beaten
2 tablespoons leeks, finely chopped,
sautéed in butter
1 tablespoon butter

Cucumber-Thyme Salad
1 small cucumber, peeled, seeded,
& finely chopped
1 teaspoon lemon thyme, finely
chopped
1 teaspoon extra virgin olive oil

Lightly dust scallops in flour. Heat oil in sauté pan. Add scallops and cook until golden, approximately 3 to 4 minutes, turning to cook on each side.

To serve, place a Smoked Salmon Cake in the center of each serving plate. Arrange 6 scallops around Smoked Salmon Cake. Top with Cucumber-Thyme Salad and drizzle with Roasted Lemon Vinaigrette. Sprinkle with chopped parsley.

Smoked Salmon Cakes: Preheat broiler.

Combine salmon and Potato Leek Cake Mix in bowl and mix gently. Shape into 4 patties.

Brush salmon cakes lightly with melted butter and place under broiler. Cook until golden brown, approximately 3 to 4 minutes.

Potato Leek Cake Mix: In saucepan, bring water to a boil. Add potato and return water to a boil; continue boiling 20 minutes. Remove from heat and allow to rest for 10 minutes.

Drain potato and cool under slowly running water for 10 minutes. Refrigerate for 30 minutes.

Peel cooled potato and shred into large bowl. Season with salt and pepper. Add egg and leeks, stir gently.

Cucumber-Thyme Salad: Mix all ingredients together in small bowl. Refrigerate until ready to use.

Roasted Lemon Vinaigrette: In blender combine lemon juice, vinegar, and mustard; process until blended. Add salt and pepper and with blender running, slowly drizzle in olive oil in a steady stream. Add fresh herbs and blend.

Roasted lemon juice: Preheat oven to 350°.

Toss lemons with salt and sugar. Place in ovenproof pan and cover with foil. Bake in oven for 45 minutes. Remove from oven; cool. Cut in half and juice.

Robert Mondavi Fume Blanc – Napa

Roasted Lemon Vinaigrette

¼ cup lemon juice, roasted*

1 tablespoon champagne vinegar

1 teaspoon Dijon mustard

¼ teaspoon kosher salt

¼ teaspoon black pepper

¼ cup olive oil

1 teaspoon fresh chives, finely chopped

1 teaspoon fresh tarragon, finely
  chopped

*Roasted lemon juice

2 whole lemons

1 tablespoon kosher salt

1 teaspoon sugar

Chilled Ceviche Cocktail

Ceviche

2	tablespoons olive oil
12	pieces jumbo shrimp, precooked, tails removed, sliced in half
¼	lb. medium size scallops, precooked
¼	lb. poached salmon, cut in 1″ pieces
½	cup plum tomatoes
¼	Spanish onion
¼	red pepper
1	jalapeño pepper, seeded & roasted
¼	cup fresh orange juice
¼	cup fresh lime juice
¼	cup cilantro, finely chopped
2	tablespoons ketchup
1	tablespoon sugar
1	teaspoon kosher salt
½	teaspoon black pepper
¼	cup mango, diced into ½″ pieces

To Serve Individual Ceviche Cocktail

¼	oz. shredded greens
½	cup ceviche
1	teaspoon mango, diced small
2	teaspoons red pepper, diced very small
1	teaspoon avocado, diced small
1	small lime wedge
6	chilled martini glasses

Ceviche: Chill shrimp, scallops, and salmon.

Preheat oven to 500°.

Roast plum tomato, onion, red and jalapeño peppers in an ovenproof pan in oven until well charred, about 15 to 20 minutes. Cool. Place cooled roasted vegetables in food processor with orange juice, lime juice, cilantro, ketchup, sugar, salt, and black pepper. Purée. Set aside.

Mix chilled seafood in medium bowl. Pour puréed mixture over seafood. Refrigerate for 24 hours.

Just prior to serving add diced mango; mix well.

To Serve Individual Ceviche Cocktail: Place shredded greens in bottom of martini glass. Top with chilled ceviche. Garnish with mango, red peppers, avocado, and fresh lime wedge.

Quivira Fig Tree Vineyard Sauvignon Blanc – Sonoma

6   portobello mushrooms, stems
       removed
     Portobello Marinade
6   portions Garlic Custard
1½ cups Parmesan Cream (see page 19)
4   teaspoons chopped chives, for
       garnish

Portobello Marinade
1   cup olive oil
2   cloves garlic
1   tablespoon fresh rosemary, finely
       chopped
1   tablespoon fresh oregano, finely
       chopped
1   tablespoon fresh basil, finely chopped
     juice of 1 lemon
2   teaspoons kosher salt
1   teaspoon black pepper
3   tablespoons balsamic vinegar
2   teaspoons soy sauce

Garlic Custard
1   cup heavy cream
6   cloves garlic, roasted (see page 25)
3   egg yolks
1   teaspoon unflavored gelatin
     pinch salt
     pinch white pepper
     pinch nutmeg
3   cloves garlic, roasted, cut in half
       (see page 25)

Mushrooms: Wash mushrooms, remove stems, and place in bowl with Portobello Marinade for 2 hours.

Preheat grill or broiler. Broil mushrooms on both sides for approximately 3 to 4 minutes. Slice mushrooms into ½″ slices.

To serve: Gently remove warm Garlic Custard from ramekin and place on individual serving plates. Arrange mushrooms slices around custard. Drizzle warm Parmesan Cream over mushrooms and custard. Sprinkle with chives.

Portobello Marinade: Place garlic and olive oil in food processor. Process until thoroughly blended. Pour into bowl with herbs, lemon juice, salt & pepper and mix well. Stir in balsamic vinegar and soy sauce.

Garlic Custard: Preheat oven to 350˚.

In small saucepan bring cream and garlic to a boil. Purée garlic-cream, egg yolks, and unflavored gelatin in food processor. Add salt, white pepper, and nutmeg. Mix well.

Place ½ of a roasted garlic clove in the center of a buttered 4 oz. ramekin. Fill ramekin to the top with garlic-cream mixture.

Place ramekin in baking pan. Fill pan with ½″ water. Bake in oven for 60 minutes, or until set. Cool.

Chateau St. Jean Pinot Noir – Sonoma

Chargrilled Scallops with Ancho-Chili Glaze

see photo SERVES **4**

20 jumbo sea scallops
Ancho-Chili Glaze
Mango Relish
1 tablespoon parsley, finely chopped

Ancho-Chili Glaze

½ cup honey
2 tablespoons Dijon mustard
2 tablespoons ancho chili powder
½ teaspoon salt
¼ teaspoon black pepper
1 teaspoon water

Mango Relish

½ mango, chopped into ½″ pieces
¼ red bell pepper, seeded, chopped into
  ½″ pieces
¼ yellow bell pepper, seeded, chopped
  into ½″ pieces
1 tablespoon red onion, diced into ¼″
  pieces
2 tablespoons pineapple juice
½ teaspoon garlic, minced
2 teaspoons fresh cilantro, finely chopped
1 tablespoon red wine vinegar
½ teaspoon curry powder
  pinch salt
  pinch black pepper
1 tablespoon extra virgin olive oil

Ancho-Chili Glaze: Combine all ingredients in mixing bowl. Refrigerate until ready to use.

Scallops: Thread scallops onto bamboo skewers. Brush with 1 tablespoon Ancho-Chile Glaze and marinate for 2 hours in refrigerator. (Reserve remaining glaze for basting and glaze.)

Preheat grill or broiler.

Place skewers on grill and cook for 5 to 6 minutes, basting several times with remaining Ancho-Chile Glaze, reserving 1 tablespoon glaze for serving.

Place ¼ cup of Mango Relish in center of serving plate. Spoon Ancho-Chili Glaze around Mango Relish. Remove scallops from skewer and arrange on plate. Garnish with chopped parsley.

Mango Relish: Combine all ingredients in bowl and mix well. Store at room temperature until ready to use.

Cline Zinfindel – California

Dungeness Crab Cakes

1   lb. Dungeness crab meat
⅓   cup dry bread crumbs
2   tablespoons red bell pepper, finely
     chopped
2   tablespoons yellow pepper, finely
     chopped
1   tablespoon inner celery rib, finely
     chopped
2   tablespoons red onion, finely
     chopped
½   teaspoon jalapeño pepper, seeded
     and finely chopped
1   egg
½   teaspoon Tabasco sauce
½   teaspoon Worcestershire sauce
¼   cup mayonnaise
4   tablespoons butter, melted
     Red Chili Mayonnaise
     chopped parsley for garnish

Red Chili Mayonnaise
¼   cup mayonnaise
¼   teaspoon Chinese Chili Paste (see
     page 202)
½   teaspoon lemon juice
1   teaspoon cold water

To prepare Crab Cakes: In mixing bowl combine crab meat and bread crumbs. Mix thoroughly; set aside.

Combine red and yellow peppers, celery, onion, jalapeño, egg, Tabasco, Worcestershire, and mayonnaise in large bowl. Fold in crab meat mixture. Form into patties; refrigerate until ready to use.

Preheat broiler.

Brush cakes with melted butter; broil on high heat until golden, approximately 3 to 5 minutes.

To serve, place on platter, drizzle with Red Chili Mayonnaise and sprinkle with chopped parsley.

Red Chili Mayonnaise: Mix all ingredients in small bowl. Refrigerate until ready to serve.

Appetizers

55

Sterling Chardonnay Diamond Mountain Ranch - Napa

6   12″ chili-cilantro tortillas (see page 202)

1   lb. skinless chicken breast, grilled & julienned into thin slices

6   tablespoons Chipotle-Red Pepper Mix

1½   cups Monterey Jack cheese, shredded

⅔   cup goat cheese

1   papaya, chopped

1   tablespoon vegetable oil to sauté tortillas
     Mango Black Bean Salsa

6   radicchio leaves

Mango Black Bean Salsa

½   lb. black beans

1   mango, diced into ½″ pieces

½   small red onion, chopped into ½″ pieces

2   tablespoons cilantro, finely chopped

2   tablespoons lime juice

2   tablespoons olive oil

1   teaspoon salt

¼   teaspoon black pepper

Chipotle-Red Pepper Mix: Roast 1 red bell pepper (see page 25). Place in plastic bag and cool.

Once cool, peel skin and place in food processor with 1 teaspoon of canned chipotle peppers, purée. Set aside until ready to serve.

Quesadilla: Brush one side of tortilla with Chipotle-Red Pepper Mix. Arrange chicken on tortilla, sprinkle with Monterey Jack cheese, goat cheese, and papaya. Fold tortilla in half.

Heat 1 tablespoon vegetable oil in medium skillet. Sauté tortilla until golden, approximately 2 to 3 minutes. Turn and sauté other side, until golden.

Cut tortilla in wedges and arrange on serving platter. Spoon Mango Black Bean Salsa into radicchio leaves and serve with tortillas.

Mango Black Bean Salsa: Soak black beans in water overnight. Drain. In saucepan, bring water to a boil. Add black beans and return to a boil. Reduce heat and simmer until beans are tender, approximately 1 hour. Drain.

Place all ingredients in bowl with black beans and mix thoroughly.

Lobster–Papaya Quesadilla

6   12″ flour tortillas
6   tablespoons Chipotle-Red Pepper Mix
3   cups Lobster-Cheese mix
6   tablespoons vegetable oil
    Mango Cream

Lobster-Cheese Mix

3   cloves garlic
¾   cup goat cheese
¾   cup Monterey Jack cheese, shredded
1   Poblano pepper, roasted, peeled,
        seeded, and finely chopped (see
        page 25)
1   red pepper, roasted, peeled, seeded,
        and finely chopped (see page 25)
1   tablespoon cilantro, finely chopped
        pinch kosher salt
1½ lbs. lobster meat, cut into ½″ pieces
1   papaya, peeled, seeded, and chopped

Mango Cream

1   mango, peeled & chopped
2   tablespoons crème fraîche
1   teaspoon lemon juice

Chipotle-Red Pepper Mix: Roast 1 red bell pepper.* Once cool, peel skin, remove seeds and membranes. Place in food processor with 1 teaspoon of canned chipotle peppers, purée.

Lobster-Cheese Mix: Preheat oven to 400°.

Place garlic in ovenproof pan and bake until golden, approximately 3 to 4 minutes. Cool; mince.

In a medium size bowl, mix garlic and all remaining ingredients together well. Set aside.

Quesadilla: Brush tortilla with Chipotle-Red Pepper Mix. Place Lobster-Cheese Mix on one side of quesadilla and fold in half.

Heat oil in ovenproof sauté pan. Place quesadilla in pan and cook until golden. Flip quesadilla, place in an ovenproof pan, continue cooking in 350° oven until golden, approximately 5 minutes.

Cut quesadilla in wedges and arrange on serving plate. Drizzle with Mango Cream.

Mango Cream: Place all ingredients in food processor and blend until thoroughly mixed. Can be stored in refrigerator for up to one week.

Appetizers

57

Grilled Shrimp with Black Bean Cakes,
Santa Fe Chili Butter, Two Tomato Salsa, & Jalapeño Cream

Appetizers

16   jumbo shrimp, tails on, peeled &
      deveined
      Santa Fe Chili Butter
4   Black Bean Cakes
      Two Tomato Salsa
      Jalapeño Cream
4   teaspoons parsley, chopped
4   bamboo skewers

Black Bean Cakes

½   lb. black beans, soaked overnight
1   tablespoon olive oil
¼   cup red onion, finely chopped
2   cloves garlic
1   jalapeño pepper, seeded, finely
      chopped
¼   cup red pepper, finely chopped
1   tablespoon honey
1   tablespoon cider vinegar
1   teaspoon chili powder
1   teaspoon ground cumin
      pinch salt
      pinch black pepper
      yellow cornmeal for dusting
2   tablespoons melted butter

Santa Fe Chili Butter

2   teaspoons butter, melted
¼   teaspoon jalapeño pepper, seeded,
      finely chopped
1   clove garlic
2   teaspoons green onion

Thread 4 shrimp on each bamboo skewer. Brush with Santa Fe Chili Butter and place under broiler or on grill. Cook for 8 to 10 minutes.

Heat Black Bean Cakes under broiler until golden, approximately 3 to 4 minutes.

To serve: Place a Black Bean Cake in the center of a serving plate. Arrange shrimp around cake. Drizzle shrimp with Santa Fe Chili Butter. Spoon Two Tomato Salsa over cake. Drizzle Jalapeño Cream over salsa. Sprinkle with chopped parsley.

Black Bean Cakes: Cover beans with enough water to cook in sauce pot. Boil and drain. Heat oil in large skillet. Add red onion, garlic, jalapeño pepper, red pepper and sauté until tender, approximately 5 minutes. Add black beans. Stir in honey, vinegar, chili powder, and cumin. Simmer over low heat until beans are very tender and liquid is absorbed, about 20 minutes.

Purée entire bean mixture in food processor. Season with salt and pepper. Transfer to a large mixing bowl and stir until mixture is thick and dry. Cool.

Form into patties. Dust lightly with yellow cornmeal. Brush with melted butter and broil until crisp and golden, approximately 3 to 4 minutes.

Santa Fe Chili Butter: Place melted butter, jalapeño, garlic, green onion, Worcestershire, and Tabasco in blender and process until thoroughly blended. Add softened butter and process until mixed. Add remaining ingredients and process thoroughly. Refrigerate until ready to use.

Two Tomato Salsa: Preheat oven to 500°.

Cut tomato in half and seed. Rub each half with olive oil. Place in baking pan and bake in oven for 15 minutes, or until tomatoes shrivel. When cool enough to handle, dice into ¼″ pieces.

Combine diced tomatoes with remaining ingredients, mix well. Refrigerate until ready to use.

Jalapeño Cream: Whip cream until it forms soft peaks. Add remaining ingredients; transfer to blender and purée until smooth. Refrigerate. Prior to serving, remove from refrigerator and allow to reach room temperature.

Ravenswood Vintner's Blend Zinfandel

¼ teaspoon Worcestershire sauce

½ teaspoon Tabasco sauce

3 tablespoons butter, softened

½ teaspoon oregano, finely chopped

½ teaspoon chili powder

pinch paprika

pinch red pepper flakes

pinch cumin

Two Tomato Salsa

1 large beefsteak tomato

1 tablespoon olive oil

2 teaspoons sun dried tomatoes, diced into ⅛″ pieces

2 teaspoons lime juice

1 clove garlic, minced

2 teaspoons fresh oregano, finely chopped

½ jalapeño pepper, seeded

¼ teaspoon kosher salt

pinch black pepper

Jalapeño Cream

1 tablespoon heavy cream

1 teaspoon sour cream

½ jalapeño pepper, seeded, finely chopped

1 teaspoon cilantro, finely chopped

pinch white pepper

squeeze of lemon juice

Grilled Polenta with Roasted Wild Mushrooms

see photo SERVES **4**

4   pieces polenta, round or 4″ squares
     (see page 26)
     Roasted Tomato Sauce
     Roasted Wild Mushrooms
4   teaspoons fresh chives, chopped

Roasted Tomato Sauce

4   plum tomatoes, halved
2   teaspoons shallots, minced
1   clove garlic
2   tablespoons olive oil
     pinch black pepper
1   sprig fresh thyme, finely chopped
1   sprig fresh chives, finely chopped
1   sprig fresh oregano, finely chopped
     pinch salt
2   teaspoons balsamic vinegar

Roasted Wild Mushrooms

10 cloves garlic, minced
4   tablespoons olive oil
4   tablespoons balsamic vinegar
4   sprigs fresh rosemary, chopped
4   sprigs fresh thyme, chopped
1   cup shitake mushrooms, sliced
1   cup oyster mushrooms, sliced
½   cup portobello mushrooms, sliced
¼   cup button mushrooms, sliced
½   teaspoon seasoning salt

Brown polenta under broiler until golden, approximately 3-5 minutes.

Ladle ¼ cup Roasted Tomato Sauce onto serving plate. Place polenta on top of sauce. Spoon Roasted Wild Mushrooms over sauce. Top with chopped chives.

Roasted Tomato Sauce: Preheat oven to 450°.

In heavy baking pan, place tomatoes, shallots, and garlic. Drizzle with olive oil. Season with black pepper and fresh herbs. Bake in oven for 30 minutes or until tomatoes are thoroughly cooked.

Remove tomatoes from oven and purée in food processor. Add salt and balsamic vinegar; purée.

Refrigerate until ready to serve.

Roasted Wild Mushrooms: Preheat oven to 450°.

In medium bowl, combine garlic, olive oil, balsamic vinegar, rosemary, and thyme. Add mushrooms and toss to coat well. Sprinkle with seasoning salt. Transfer to baking sheet and roast in oven for 25 minutes.

Robert Sinskey Pinot Noir – Los Carneros

Fried Catfish Fingers

1½ lbs. catfish, cut into 24 strips
2 cups vegetable oil
12 slices green tomatoes, ½″ thick
⅔ cup Remoulade Sauce
6 teaspoons chopped parsley
Louisiana Cajun Batter for dusting
Buttermilk for soaking

Green Tomatoes

3 green tomatoes
½ cup flour for dusting
2 eggs
½ cup yellow cornmeal for dusting

Remoulade Sauce

½ cup mayonnaise
2 tablespoons celery, chopped fine
1 tablespoon green onions, chopped fine
2 teaspoons parsley, chopped fine
1 teaspoon horseradish
1½ teaspoons Creole mustard
1½ teaspoons ketchup
1½ teaspoons Lea and Perrins Sauce®
1 teaspoon capers, chopped fine
1 teaspoon sweet gherkins, chopped fine
1 teaspoon mustard
1 teaspoon Tabasco sauce
1 teaspoon garlic, chopped fine
½ teaspoon paprika
¼ teaspoon salt
¼ teaspoon lemon juice

Louisiana Cajun Batter

½ cup cracker meal
½ cup Fry Krisp® batter mix
1 tablespoon Cajun spice blend

To Prepare Catfish: Soak catfish in buttermilk for 1 hour, dust in Cajun Batter. Heat oil in sauté pan; add catfish (4 pieces) and cook until golden brown, about 5-6 minutes. Keep catfish warm in oven. Heat additional oil in sauté pan and add tomatoes and cook on both sides until golden, about 2-3 minutes on each side. Place 2 tomatoes on a serving plate, and place catfish on top of tomatoes. Drizzle Remoulade Sauce on top of catfish and top with chopped parsley.

Green Tomatoes: Slice tomatoes ½″ thick, dust in flour, dredge in egg wash, and coat with yellow cornmeal.

Remoulade Sauce: Place ½ of the mayonnaise in a blender with all of the remaining ingredients and emulsify well. Pour into a mixing bowl, add the remaining mayonnaise, and mix well. Refrigerate until ready to use.

Louisiana Cajun Batter: Mix all together well.

Soups

IN THE FOLLOWING CHAPTER I'VE INCLUDED SEVERAL SOUPS THAT
WE SERVE DURING THE COURSE OF THE FALL AND WINTER. OUR
SEAFOOD CHOWDER HAS BEEN A SIGNATURE SOUP SINCE DAY ONE.
ALL OF THESE ARE GREAT TO MAKE ON ANY OCCASION. THERE'S
NOTHING LIKE A BOWL OF HOT SOUP AND CRUSTY BREAD ON A
COLD WINTER DAY.

Pinconning Cheese Soup

¼ cup bacon, chopped fine
⅔ cup onion, chopped fine
¼ cup celery, chopped fine
¼ cup carrots, chopped fine
2 tablespoons flour
⅛ teaspoon nutmeg
⅛ teaspoon white pepper
1 quart Chicken Stock (see page 23)
1 cup half-and-half
1 lb. Pinconning cheese, shredded
1 tablespoon parsley, chopped fine

Cook bacon in soup pot until crispy. Add onion, celery, and carrots and cook until soft. Add flour and seasonings, cook, stirring for two minutes. Add Chicken Stock, bring to a boil, reduce heat, and simmer for 30 minutes. Stir in half-and-half and shredded cheese, mix well. Cook until cheese is melted and soup is thickened. Add chopped parsley and mix well.

Serve hot.

Roasted Three Onion Soup

4 tablespoons olive oil
2 yellow onions, sliced thin
2 red onions, sliced thin
1 stalk leek, sliced thin
3 cloves garlic, minced
1 cup Brown Chicken Stock (see page 23)
4 cups Beef Stock (see page 24)
¼ cup dark beer
½ cup cooking sherry
   toasted croutons
   Cheese Topping

Cheese Topping
½ cup Parmesan cheese, shredded
1 cup Gruyère cheese, shredded

Preheat oven to 400°.

Pour olive oil in bottom of 9x13″ pan. Evenly spread onions and leeks in bottom of pan and bake for 45-60 minutes, or until onions are golden. Add garlic and mix well. Return pan to oven for an additional 15 minutes. Remove from oven and set aside.

In large soup pot bring Brown Chicken Stock and Beef Stock to a boil. Add cooked onions and stir. Add beer and cooking sherry and continue cooking for 30 minutes. Remove from stove.

Preheat broiler.

Pour 8 oz. of soup into four ovenproof crocks. Top with toasted croutons and Cheese Topping. Place under broiler until cheese is bubbly and golden, approximately 3 to 5 minutes.

Serve hot.

Smoked Chicken, Sweet Potato, & Corn Chowder

6	strips bacon, chopped fine
1	lg. Spanish onion, diced
½	cup butter
1	teaspoon fresh basil
1	teaspoon fresh thyme
½	cup flour
4	ears corn, kernels removed (about 2 cups)
1	red pepper, diced
1	lb. sweet potatoes, diced & blanched
1	cup water
6	cups Chicken Stock (see page 23)
2	lbs. Smoked Chicken (see page 26), diced
1½	cups milk
1	tablespoon salt
¼	teaspoon black pepper
1	tablespoon parsley, chopped fine

Cook bacon in large soup pot until crispy. Add onion, butter, basil, and thyme. Cook until onion is soft, approximately 5 minutes. Add flour and mix well. Stir in corn, red pepper and sweet potatoes; sauté for 5 minutes. Add water, Chicken Stock and Smoked Chicken and bring to a boil. Stir in milk, salt and pepper and return to a boil. Continue cooking until soup has thickened. Stir in chopped parsley.

Serve hot.

New England Seafood Chowder

1	cup water
1½	lbs. potatoes, diced into ½″ pieces
5	strips bacon, chopped into small pieces
1½	lbs. onions, chopped fine
2	ribs of celery, chopped fine
1	green pepper, julienned into thin strips
½	cup butter
½	cup flour
6	cups Fish Stock (see page 24)
1	tablespoon parsley, chopped fine
1	14 oz. can Progresso® clams, chopped
½	lb. large shrimp, peeled & deveined
½	lb. scallops, halved
2	cups milk

Place water and potatoes in soup pot, and bring to a boil.

In medium pan, sauté bacon until crispy. Add onions and sauté until translucent, approximately 5 minutes. Repeat with celery and green pepper. Add butter and flour and mix well. Cook for 3-4 minutes.

Transfer bacon/vegetable mixture to soup pot with potatoes and water. Mix thoroughly. Stir in Fish Stock and parsley. Add clams, shrimp, and scallops. Bring to a boil and cook for 30 minutes.

Stir in milk and continue cooking for 15 minutes or until chowder thickens. Remove from heat.

Serve hot.

Seafood Chowder

2   tablespoons olive oil

2   cloves garlic, minced

1   large onion, chopped fine

1   small leek, sliced into ¼″ pieces

2   ribs of celery, chopped fine

1   teaspoon fresh oregano

1   teaspoon fresh basil

½   teaspoon fresh thyme

2   teaspoons fennel seeds

1   28 oz. can Italian plum tomatoes, diced

2   cups water

½   lb. fish fillets, such as cod, sea bass, or
        whitefish

1   14 oz. can Progresso® clams, chopped

½   lb. scallops

½   lb. shrimp pieces, peeled and deveined

4   cups Fish Stock (see page 24)

1   teaspoon saffron

¼   teaspoon cayenne pepper

1   tablespoon cooking sherry

2   teaspoons salt

1   tablespoon parsley

Heat olive oil in large soup pot until hot. Add garlic and sauté until golden. Add onion, leek, celery, oregano, basil, thyme, & fennel seeds. Cook for approximately 25 to 30 minutes, or until golden. Add tomatoes and cook for 15 minutes.

Add water, fish fillets, and chopped clams and continue cooking, uncovered, for 30 minutes. Stir occasionally to break up fish. Add scallops, shrimp, Fish Stock, saffron, cayenne pepper, and cooking sherry. Cook for 30 minutes. Add salt and parsley. Mix well.

Serve hot.

Black Bean Soup

1   lb. black beans

6   cups water

6   strips bacon, chopped into medium
      size pieces

1   small onion, chopped fine

2   ribs of celery, chopped fine

1   clove garlic, minced

2   teaspoons cayenne pepper

2   teaspoons black pepper

2   tablespoons salt

1   tablespoon cornstarch

½   lb. smoked ham, diced into ¼″ pieces

1   tomato, diced

     Fresh Tomato Salsa, for topping (see
      page 21)

     Jalapeño Cream, for topping (see
      page 59)

     green onions, chopped for garnish

Soak black beans in water overnight. Rinse well. Drain. Place beans in a large soup pot with 6 cups water. Cover and bring to a slow boil.

Sauté bacon in saucepan until crisp. Add onion, celery, and garlic and cook until translucent. Stir in cayenne pepper and black pepper; mix well. Add salt, cornstarch, and diced ham, cook for 1 minute. Transfer to soup pot with beans. Stir in diced tomato and cook over low heat for 1 hour, or until beans are tender.

Serve in individual bowls topped with Tomato Salsa, and a dollop of Jalapeño Cream, and chopped green onions.

Serve hot.

New England Clam Chowder

2	cups water
1½	lbs. potatoes, diced
6	strips bacon, cut into small pieces
1	tablespoon oregano
1	tablespoon basil
2	onions, chopped fine
2	ribs of celery, chopped fine
2	carrots, chopped fine
⅓	cup butter
⅓	cup flour
2	cups Fish Stock (see page 24)
2	14 oz. cans Progresso® clams, chopped
2	cups milk
1	tablespoon parsley, chopped

Bring water to a boil in soup pot. Add potatoes and continue to boil until potatoes are tender, approximately 20 minutes.

In medium pan, sauté bacon until crispy. Stir in oregano and basil. Add onions and sauté until translucent, approximately 3 to 4 minutes. Add celery and carrots and continue cooking until tender, approximately 5 minutes. Add butter and flour and mix well. Cook for 3-4 minutes.

Transfer sautéed vegetable/herb mixture to stockpot with water and potatoes. Add Fish Stock and clams. Bring to a boil.

Thoroughly blend in milk and continue cooking for 5-10 minutes, or until soup is thick. Add parsley. Remove from heat.

Serve hot.

Lemon Chicken & Wild Rice Soup

½ cup butter

1 small onion, diced fine

2 ribs of celery, diced fine

1 teaspoon fresh thyme

½ red bell pepper, diced into ¼″ pieces

¼ cup flour

1 cup water

6 cups Chicken Stock (see page 23)

½ lb. chicken meat, diced into ½″ pieces

¼ lb. wild rice blend, cooked

3 tablespoons lemon juice

1 cup milk

1 tablespoon parsley, chopped

In medium pan, slowly melt butter over low heat until hot. Add onion and sauté until translucent, approximately 5 minutes. Add celery and continue cooking until tender. Add thyme and red pepper, mix well and cook for 3-4 minutes. Add flour, mix well, and cook for 3-4 minutes.

Place water in soup pot. Add Chicken Stock and sautéed vegetable mixture. Add chicken, wild rice, lemon juice, and milk. Bring to a boil, and continue cooking until soup is thickened. Sprinkle in chopped parsley, mix well. Remove from heat.

Serve hot.

Chicken Tortilla Soup

1½   tablespoons olive oil
1   small red onion, diced
1   clove garlic, minced
¼   lb. carrots, diced
2   ribs of celery, diced
½   large red pepper, diced
½   large yellow pepper, diced
1   Poblano chili pepper, diced
1   teaspoon fresh oregano
1   teaspoon cumin
1   tablespoon kosher salt
¼   teaspoon black pepper
¼   teaspoon red pepper flakes
1   28 oz. can Italian plum tomatoes, chopped
5   cups Chicken Stock (see page 23)
1   lb. chicken, cooked & diced
6   6″ corn tortillas, cut in thin strips, fried for garnish
     Cheese Topping, for garnish

Cheese Topping
½   cup Monterey Jack cheese, shredded
½   tablespoon cilantro, chopped
½   tablespoon lemon zest

Heat olive oil in soup pot. Add red onion and cook until translucent, approximately 5 minutes. Add garlic and cook for 3 to 4 minutes. Stir in carrots and celery and cook until carrots are soft, approximately 6 to 8 minutes. Thoroughly mix in peppers, oregano, cumin, salt, black pepper, and red pepper flakes.

Stir in tomatoes and Chicken Stock and cook for 30 minutes. Add diced chicken and continue cooking for an additional 30 minutes.

To serve, ladle soup into bowl and top with fried corn tortilla strips and cheese mixture.

Cheese Topping: In small bowl, combine all ingredients; mix well.

Corn tortilla strips: Cut corn tortillas into thin strips. Heat 1 tablespoon olive oil in sauté pan. Sauté tortilla strips until crispy, approximately 3 to 4 minutes. Remove from pan and place on paper towel until ready to serve.

Serve hot.

Lamb, Mushroom, & Barley Soup

¼ cup barley
1 tablespoon vegetable oil
2 cloves garlic, minced
1 large onion, diced medium
2 carrots, chopped medium
1 parsnip, chopped medium
½ lb. mushrooms, sliced thick
1 lb. lamb stew meat, cut in 1″ cubes
6 cups Beef Stock (see page 24)
1 cup water
3 tablespoons tomato paste
2 teaspoons salt
¼ teaspoon black pepper
1 tablespoon parsley, chopped fine

Soak barley in water for 30 minutes.

Heat oil in soup pot. Add garlic and cook for 1 minute. Add onion and cook until translucent, approximately 5 minutes. Stir in carrots and parsnip and cook until tender, about 8 minutes. Add mushrooms, lamb, Beef Stock and water; bring to a boil. Drain barley and add to soup mixture along with tomato paste, salt, and black pepper. Continue cooking for an additional 15 minutes. Remove from heat.

Garnish with parsley. Serve hot.

Salads & Salad Dressings

THE ENTRÉE SALADS THAT I HAVE CHOSEN FOR THE BOOK ARE THE ONES I'M PARTICULARLY FOND OF. THE DUCK SALAD AND THE SMOKED CHICKEN ARE MY FAVORITES. THE GRILLED SALMON SALAD IS EXCELLENT ON A SUMMER DAY.

3   cured duck breasts*, 10-12 ounces each

6   cups Mesclun salad greens mix

1   yellow pepper, julienned

1   red pepper, julienned

    Port Wine Vinaigrette

3   Honey Pears

    Carmelized Pecans

1   cup Laura Chenel® goat cheese, crumbled

*Cured Duck (requires a 24 hour rest)

3   duck breasts

1   cup water

1   tablespoon sugar

1   tablespoon brown sugar

1   tablespoon kosher salt

1   bay leaf

2   juniper berries, crushed

1   sprig fresh thyme

Port Wine Vinaigrette

½   cup port wine

¼   cup apricot jam

1   teaspoon lime zest

1   teaspoon orange zest

½   cup olive oil

¼   cup balsamic vinegar

½   teaspoon kosher salt

    pinch black pepper

Honey Pears

3   pears, ripe, sliced into 12 pieces each

¼   cup honey

Carmelized Pecans

¼   cup sugar

2   tablespoons water

½   cup pecan halves

Cured Duck: Trim excess fat from duck. Score the skin of each breast without cutting into flesh. Place duck in a plastic container and add all cured duck ingredients. Cover and allow to rest for 24 hours. Prior to preparation, rinse duck well.

Pan sear duck breasts to medium rare. Slice on bias into very thin pieces. Set aside.

Place salad greens and peppers in large bowl and toss with 1 cup of Port Wine Vinaigrette. Transfer greens to 6 individual serving plates.

Place 6 pieces of Honey Pear in a pinwheel on each salad. Arrange duck slices around the pear. Sprinkle with Carmelized Pecans and goat cheese. Drizzle with remaining Port Wine Vinaigrette.

Port Wine Vinaigrette: In a small saucepan, combine port wine, jam, lime and orange zest, and cook over medium heat until jam is melted. Increase heat and continue cooking until mixture boils. Reduce heat and continue cooking over low heat until mixture is reduced by half.

Thoroughly blend in olive oil, balsamic vinegar, salt, and pepper. Refrigerate.

Honey Pears: Place pears and honey in a large sauté pan and cook over medium heat until pears turn a golden color and liquid has evaporated.

Carmelized Pecans: Combine sugar and water in a sauté pan and cook until mixture begins to turn amber. Stir in pecans, making certain they are well coated with sugar mixture. Continue cooking until pecans become carmelized. Remove from heat and cool on a sheet tray lined with parchment or waxed paper. Store at room temperature.

Bethel Heights Pinot Noir – Oregon

At The Common Grill we prepare it with Indiana duck, but a California Sonoma duck is also an excellent choice.

Black Bean Salad

1	lb. black beans
2	cloves garlic, minced
½	cup red onion, finely chopped
¼	cup red pepper, diced into ½″ pieces
2	tablespoons yellow pepper, diced into ½″ pieces
1	tablespoon parsley, finely chopped
2	tablespoons cilantro, finely chopped
1	tablespoon green onion, finely chopped
1	teaspoon fresh thyme, finely chopped
2	teaspoons cumin
	pinch cayenne pepper
	pinch salt
	pinch cracked black pepper
¼	cup olive oil
1	tablespoon lime juice
1	tablespoon sherry wine
1	tablespoon balsamic vinegar
1	head radicchio

Soak beans in water overnight. Rinse and drain.

Slowly cook beans in stockpot until tender, approximately 1 hour. Drain. Set aside.

Meanwhile, in large bowl combine all remaining ingredients, except radicchio, and mix well. Add beans and stir. Refrigerate.

Separate leaves carefully from head of radicchio without tearing or breaking, and rinse. Line serving plate with radicchio leaves and place Black Bean Salad on top.

6   pieces Goat Cheese Croutons
30 jumbo shrimp, deveined, peeled,
        tails on
½   lb. angel hair pasta, cooked
1½ cups Mesclun salad greens mix
        Key Lime-Mango Vinaigrette

Key Lime-Mango Vinaigrette

3   mangoes, puréed
1   tablespoon garlic, minced
2   ounces key lime juice
1   mango, peeled & diced into ¼″
        pieces
8   ounces olive oil
2   ounces champagne vinegar
1   teaspoon kosher salt
½   teaspoon black pepper
1   tablespoon fresh basil, chopped

Goat Cheese Croutons

    loaf of French bread
1   package (5.3 oz.) goat cheese
¼   cup olive oil

Place shrimp in a steamer basket over boiling water and steam until shrimp turns pink, approximately 3 to 4 minutes. Remove from heat and cool.

In a medium bowl, toss angel hair pasta with ½ cup vinaigrette. Set aside.

In a separate bowl, toss salad greens with remaining vinaigrette. Divide evenly onto individual serving plates. Arrange 5 shrimp on each salad.

Divide the angel hair pasta into six portions and twirl each portion on a fork. Gently slide pasta off the fork into the center of each salad. Serve with a Goat Cheese Crouton.

Key Lime-Mango Vinaigrette: Peel the mangoes. Place in the bowl of a food processor, fitted with the metal blade, along with the garlic and key lime juice. Process until mixture is puréed. Transfer mixture to a medium bowl. Add all remaining ingredients and mix well.

Goat Cheese Croutons: Slice bread on bias into ¾″ slices. Spread goat cheese evenly over top of bread. Drizzle with olive oil. Just prior to serving, place in a warm oven for 5 minutes.

Salads & Salad Dressings

81

Turnbull Sauvignon Blanc - Oakville

Grilled Salmon Salad with Ginger Citrus Vinaigrette

6   6 oz. pieces salmon
24   spears asparagus
6   cups Mesclun salad greens mix
24   orange sections
1   red bell pepper, julienned fine
     Ginger-Citrus Vinaigrette

Ginger-Citrus Vinaigrette
2   tablespoons lemon juice
2   tablespoons orange juice
2   tablespoons ginger purée
3   cloves garlic, roasted (see page 25)
1   cup olive oil
4   tablespoons red onion, chopped
4   tablespoons raspberry vinegar
1   teaspoon salt
1   tablespoon chives, chopped

Grill salmon. Set aside.

In a saucepan, bring water to a boil. Add asparagus spears and blanch for 1 minute. Drain and cool.

In a large bowl, toss asparagus, salad greens, orange sections, and pepper with 1 cup of vinaigrette.

Remove asparagus spears from mixture. Arrange 4 spears of asparagus in a pinwheel on each serving plate. Divide salad greens evenly and mound on top of asparagus. Place a piece of salmon on the side of each salad. Drizzle remaining vinaigrette equally over each salad.

Ginger-Citrus Vinaigrette: Place all ingredients, except chives, in a blender and purée. Transfer mixture to a bowl and add chives.

Dry Creek Fume Blanc – Sonoma

12   cups Mesclun salad greens mix
      Sweet Balsamic Vinaigrette
2   yellow peppers, roasted & julienned
         (see page 25)
2   red peppers, roasted & julienned (see
         page 25)
3   portobello mushrooms, grilled & sliced
18   pieces Gorgonzola Polenta Croutons
24   Calamata olives
6   tablespoons sun dried tomatoes

Gorgonzola Polenta Croutons

1½   cups water
2½   cups vegetable stock
2   teaspoons, garlic, minced
1½   cups yellow cornmeal
1   cup sour cream
⅓   cup Parmesan cheese, shredded
½   cup Gorgonzola cheese, crumbled
¼   cup butter
1   teaspoon kosher salt
¼   teaspoon white pepper
      flour, for dusting
1   tablespoon olive oil

Sweet Balsamic Vinaigrette

1½   cups olive oil
½   cup white balsamic vinegar
2   teaspoons garlic, minced
2   tablespoons sugar
2   tablespoons dry mustard
2   teaspoons kosher salt
1   teaspoon cracked black pepper

Place salad greens in a large bowl and toss with Sweet Balsamic Vinaigrette. Divide among six individual serving plates.

Distribute yellow peppers, red peppers, and Portobello mushrooms over each salad. Top with Gorgonzola Polenta Croutons, Calamata olives, and sun dried tomatoes.

Gorgonzola Polenta Croutons: Preheat oven to 350°.

In a large ovenproof saucepan, bring water, vegetable stock, and garlic to a boil. Stir in cornmeal, reduce heat and continue cooking for 5 minutes, stirring constantly. Cover and transfer to oven and bake for 30 minutes.

Remove from oven and stir in sour cream, cheeses, butter, salt, and pepper. Pour mixture onto greased cookie sheet. Cool.

Cut into crouton size pieces. Dust in flour.

Heat 1 tablespoon olive oil in sauté pan. Place croutons in pan and sauté until golden, approximately 2 to 3 minutes.

Sweet Balsamic Vinaigrette: Combine all ingredients in a bowl and mix thoroughly. Refrigerate until ready to serve.

Byron Pinot Gris

Asian Chicken Salad

see photo | SERVES **4**

4   6-8 oz. pieces chicken breast, skinless
      Honey Sesame Vinaigrette
6   cups Mesclun salad greens mix
2   cups napa cabbage, sliced into
      2″ pieces
2   red peppers, julienned fine
2   yellow peppers, julienned fine
4   tablespoons green onions, sliced
      on bias
½   cup carrots, julienned fine
½   cup daikon radish, julienned fine
½   cup pea pods
½   cup honey roasted peanuts, chopped
½   cup fried rice-stick noodles

Honey Sesame Vinaigrette

⅓   cup rice wine vinegar
3   tablespoons teriyaki sauce
⅓   cup sesame oil
2   tablespoons grated ginger
⅓   cup honey
1   tablespoon sesame seeds, toasted
2   teaspoons minced garlic
1   tablespoon Hoisin sauce (see
      page 202)
2   tablespoons lemon juice
2   teaspoons hot chili oil
2   tablespoons peanut oil

Marinate chicken breast in half of the Honey Sesame Vinaigrette for one hour. Grill. Set aside.

Place greens and all remaining vegetables in large bowl; add other half of vinaigrette and toss well.

Divide salad greens onto 4 individual serving plates. Slice chicken breasts and arrange on each salad. Sprinkle with honey roasted peanuts and fried rice-stick noodles.

Honey Sesame Vinaigrette: Combine all ingredients in a medium bowl and mix thoroughly.

Honey Pecan Chicken Salad

1 tablespoon honey
  Mustard Sauce
⅔ cup mayonnaise
2 tablespoons onions, minced
2 tablespoons celery, diced fine
2 lbs. chicken breasts, cooked & diced
   into ½″ pieces
1 tablespoon parsley, minced
4 tablespoons pecans, toasted
2 Granny Smith apples, chopped into
   ½″ pieces
3 cups Mesclun salad greens mix
6 red & yellow teardrop tomatoes, halved
6 teaspoons pecans, chopped (for
   topping)
  fresh fruit for garnish

Mustard Sauce

⅓ cup mayonnaise
1 ounce Grey Poupon® mustard
½ teaspoon dry mustard
¼ teaspoon lemon juice

In a medium bowl, thoroughly mix honey, Mustard Sauce, and mayonnaise. Stir in onions, celery, chicken, parsley, pecans, and apples. Refrigerate until ready to serve.

Divide salad greens evenly among six serving plates. Top each with chicken salad. Arrange tomatoes on plate and sprinkle with chopped pecans. Garnish with fresh fruit.

Mustard Sauce: Place all ingredients in a small bowl and mix well.

Salads & Salad Dressings

Pine Ridge Chenin Blanc – Napa

Smoked Chicken Salad with
Lemon Hazelnut Vinaigrette

see photo | SERVES 6

12 cups Mesclun salad greens mix
12 radicchio leaves, julienned
   Lemon Hazelnut Vinaigrette
24 pieces Grilled Honey Pears
1 lb. smoked chicken breast, sliced
   (see page 202 or page 26)
⅔ cup feta cheese
6 tablespoons hazelnuts, toasted &
   chopped fine

Grilled Honey Pears
3 yellow Bartlett pears
½ cup water
   squeeze of lemon juice
2 ounces honey
2 ounces butter, melted

Lemon Hazelnut Vinaigrette
1 tablespoon lemon zest
¼ cup lemon juice
1 tablespoon garlic, minced
1 teaspoon kosher salt
¼ teaspoon black pepper
2 teaspoons Dijon mustard
⅓ cup rice wine vinegar
⅓ cup peanut oil
1 cup extra virgin olive oil
2 tablespoons parsley, chopped
1 tablespoon hazelnuts, toasted
   & chopped

In a large bowl, combine salad greens, radicchio, and vinaigrette. Toss to coat. Divide evenly among 6 individual serving plates.

Arrange 4 pieces of Grilled Honey Pears on each salad, followed by smoked chicken.

Sprinkle with feta cheese and hazelnuts.

Grilled Honey Pears: Core and quarter pears. Soak in water and lemon juice until ready to use. Drain.

In a separate medium bowl, combine honey and butter. Add pear quarters and toss to coat.

Grill or broil for 5 to 6 minutes, until grilled on all sides.

Lemon Hazelnut Vinaigrette: Place lemon zest, lemon juice, garlic, salt, pepper, Dijon mustard, and rice wine vinegar in a blender and process until well blended.

In a slow, steady stream, add both oils to blender and process until slightly thickened.

Transfer mixture to medium bowl and stir in parsley and hazelnuts.

Refrigerate until ready to serve.

Hess Select Chardonnay - California

Tuna Salad Nicoise

see photo | SERVES **4**

4   6 oz. pieces Ahi tuna
     Tuna Marinade
1   tablespoon olive oil
4   cups Mesclun salad greens mix
16 oil-cured black olives, pitted
¼   lb. French beans, trimmed & blanched
¼   lb. yellow beans, trimmed & blanched
4   redskin potatoes, quartered & steamed
12 spears asparagus, trimmed & blanched
8   red cherry tomatoes, halved
8   yellow cherry tomatoes, halved
¼   lb. ricotta salada or feta cheese, crumbled
     Roasted Lemon-Basil Vinaigrette

Tuna Marinade

½   cup extra virgin olive oil
1   sprig rosemary, chopped
1   sprig thyme, chopped
1   sprig oregano, chopped
1   tablespoon fennel seed, crushed
¼   teaspoon kosher salt
     pinch black pepper

Roasted Lemon-Basil Vinaigrette

⅓   cup Roasted Lemon Juice
4   tablespoons champagne vinegar
1   tablespoon Dijon mustard
1   teaspoon kosher salt
¼   teaspoon black pepper
1½ cups olive oil
1½ teaspoons fresh chives, finely chopped
1   tablespoon fresh basil, finely chopped

Roasted Lemon Juice

6   whole lemons
⅓   cup kosher salt
1½ teaspoons sugar

Marinate tuna in the Tuna Marinade and refrigerate overnight.

Heat olive oil in sauté pan. Sear tuna on all sides until medium rare, approximately 6-8 minutes, or until cooked to personal taste. Remove from pan and set aside.

Mix salad greens with ½ cup vinaigrette. Divide onto serving plates.

Slice tuna in ½″ slices and arrange on salad greens.

In a large bowl, toss olives, beans, potatoes, asparagus, and tomatoes with remaining vinaigrette. Pour evenly over top of sliced tuna.

Sprinkle with cheese.

Tuna Marinade: Combine all ingredients in bowl; mix thoroughly. Refrigerate until ready to use.

Roasted Lemon-Basil Vinaigrette: Combine Roasted Lemon Juice, vinegar, and mustard in a bowl; mix thoroughly. Stir in salt and pepper.

    Using a wire whisk, slowly pour in olive oil in a steady stream, whisking constantly to blend. Stir in fresh herbs.

Roasted Lemon Juice: Preheat oven to 350°.

Toss lemons with salt and sugar. Place in an ovenproof pan. Cover.

Bake in oven for 45 minutes. Remove from oven; cool.

When cool, cut lemons in half, and juice.

La Famiglia Di Mondavi Pinot Grigio

Grilled Chicken Salad

6 6-8 oz. pieces skinless chicken breast
12 asparagus spears
12 cups Mesclun salad greens mix
2 Granny Smith apples, peeled & diced
     into ½″ pieces
1 zucchini, juilenned fine
1 small carrot, julienned fine
1 red pepper, julienned into ¼″ slices
1 cucumber, peeled, seeded & cut on bias
6 tablespoons pecans, toasted & chopped
    Honey Bacon Vinaigrette

Honey Bacon Vinaigrette
5 strips bacon
⅔ cup olive oil
½ cup honey
⅓ cup lemon juice
2 tablespoons Hoisin sauce (see
     page 202)
1 clove garlic
2 tablespoons Dijon mustard
2 teaspoons black pepper
2 teaspoons basil, chopped

Grill chicken breast. Cut on bias into ½″ slices. Set aside.

Blanch asparagus spears in boiling water for one minute. Set aside and let cool.

Combine salad greens, apples, zucchini, carrots, red pepper, cucumber, and asparagus in a large bowl. Add vinaigrette and mix well.

Divide salad greens evenly among six serving plates. Arrange chicken slices on each salad. Top with chopped pecans.

Honey Bacon Vinaigrette: Cook bacon until crispy. Reserve bacon grease. When cool enough to handle, chop bacon into small pieces. Set aside.

Place olive oil, honey, lemon juice, Hoisin sauce, garlic, and Dijon mustard into blender. Add bacon grease. Process until thoroughly blended.

Transfer to mixing bowl and add bacon pieces, pepper, and basil.

Refrigerate until ready to serve.

Chappellet Chenin Blanc - Napa

Raspberry-Maple Vinaigrette

½	cup raspberry vinegar
½	cup olive oil
½	cup peanut oil
½	cup maple syrup
1	tablespoon Dijon mustard
1	tablespoon tarragon leaves, crumbled
1	teaspoon salt

Place all ingredients in a bowl and whisk until well blended.

Makes approximately 2 cups

Raspberry-Maple Vinaigrette is our house dressing. I created it while an Executive Chef for the Chuck Muer restaurants in 1983. My guests at The Common Grill rave about it!

Salsa Vinaigrette

⅔	cup Fresh Tomato Salsa (see page 21)
1	clove garlic
2	tablespoons red wine vinegar
2	tablespoons lemon juice
¼	teaspoon cumin
1	tablespoon parsley
1	tablespoon jalapeño pepper, halved & seeded
¼	cup olive oil

Place salsa, garlic, vinegar, lemon juice, cumin, parsley and jalapeño pepper in blender and process until well blended.

In a slow steady stream, add olive oil and process until well blended.

Refrigerate until ready to serve.

Makes approximately 1 cup

This goes well on any Southwestern type of salad.

Dijon-Poppy Seed Vinaigrette

2 cups vegetable oil ¼ cup red wine vinegar ½ cup Dijon mustard 3 tablespoons honey 4 tablespoons poppy seeds 2 teaspoons salt	Place all ingredients in a bowl and whisk until well blended. Refrigerate until ready to serve. **Makes approximately 3 cups**

Herb-Balsamic Vinaigrette

2 tablespoons Dijon mustard 1¼ cups olive oil ⅓ cup balsamic vinegar 1 tablespoon fresh chives, finely chopped 1 teaspoon fresh thyme, stems removed & finely chopped 1 teaspoon fresh basil, finely chopped pinch salt pinch black pepper	Combine all ingredients in a bowl and whisk until well blended. Refrigerate until ready to serve. **Makes approximately 2 cups**

Pesto Vinaigrette

2	cups fresh basil, packed
6	cloves garlic
8	tablespoons Parmesan cheese, grated
4	teaspoons pine nuts
1	cup olive oil
3	oz. Balsamic vinegar

Place all ingredients in a blender and process until well blended.

Refrigerate until ready to serve.

Makes approximately 1½ cups

This is great tossed in a potato salad.

Blue Cheese Dressing

2	cups mayonnaise
4	tablespoons cider vinegar
¼	cup Wesson® oil
2	tablespoons sour cream
1	teaspoon lemon juice
¼	cup water
½	teaspoon dry mustard
¼	teaspoon salt
	pinch white pepper
8	ounces Maytag® Blue Cheese, crumbled

In a medium bowl, mix together mayonnaise, cider vinegar, Wesson® oil, sour cream, lemon juice and water.

Blend in dry mustard, salt and pepper.

Add blue cheese and mix well

Makes approximately 3 cups

Honey Sesame Vinaigrette

½	cup rice wine vinegar
¼	cup teriyaki sauce
½	cup sesame oil
2	tablespoons ginger, grated
½	cup honey
½	tablespoon garlic, minced
1	tablespoon Hoisin sauce (see page 202)
2	tablespoons lemon juice
½	tablespoon hot chili oil
2	tablespoons peanut oil

Combine all ingredients in a bowl and whisk until well blended.

Makes approximately 2 cups

Lemon, Mustard, Chive Vinaigrette

2	tablespoons lemon juice
4	teaspoons Dijon mustard
1	tablespoon balsamic vinegar
1	cup olive oil
½	cup chives, chopped
	black pepper to taste
¼	teaspoon salt

In a blender, combine lemon juice, Dijon mustard, and balsamic vinegar. Slowly add olive oil until thickened. Remove from blender and add chives, black pepper, and salt. Keep refrigerated.

Makes approximately 1 cup

Brunch

WE STARTED SERVING BRUNCH THE SECOND YEAR WE WERE OPEN AND HAVE HAD GREAT SUCCESS. THE FOLLOWING ARE SOME MENU ITEMS PAST AND PRESENT THAT WE'VE ENJOYED PREPARING FOR OUR GUESTS. THE APPLE PRALINE FRENCH TOAST AND THE MASA CORNCAKES ARE REAL TREATS TO HAVE ON A LAZY SUNDAY MORNING.

Lemon Waffles with Blackberry Butter

SERVES 6

1½ cups all-purpose flour
¼ teaspoon salt
2 teaspoons baking powder
2 tablespoons baking soda
2 teaspoons lemon zest
3 tablespoons butter, melted
3 eggs, separated
1½ cups milk
2 teaspoons vanilla
Blackberry Butter
fresh berries for garnish
powdered sugar for garnish

Blackberry Butter
1 stick butter, softened
1 cup Blackberry Sauce

Blackberry Sauce
1 lb. blackberries
¼ cup sugar
1 tablespoon Grand Marnier® liqueur, optional
1 teaspoon lemon juice

To prepare waffles: Sift dry ingredients into large bowl. Stir in lemon zest. Set aside.

In small bowl mix together melted butter, egg yolks, milk, and vanilla. Add to flour mixture.

In a separate large bowl, beat egg whites until soft peaks form. Gently fold in waffle batter.

Pour 1 cup of batter onto hot waffle iron and cook until golden for each waffle.

Top with ¼ cup Blackberry Butter and fresh berries. Serve with warm maple syrup and sprinkle with powdered sugar.

Blackberry Butter: In small bowl blend together butter and blackberry sauce.

Blackberry Sauce: Place all ingredients in blender and purée. Strain to remove seeds.

Brunch

98

Stuffed French Toast

6   pieces egg bread, 1″ thick
2   tablespoons powdered sugar, for
        garnish
     maple syrup

Streusel Topping

½   cup toasted, sliced almonds
¼   cup brown sugar
¾   cup rolled oats
½   cup flour
1   teaspoon cinnamon
4   tablespoons butter, softened

Batter

1   cup milk
3   eggs, beaten
¼   teaspoon cinnamon
⅛   teaspoon vanilla
¼   cup sugar

French Toast Stuffing

4   tablespoons butter
¼   cup sugar
2   tablespoons water
6   ripe bananas, mashed
1½   cups peaches, sliced & peeled

Streusel Topping: Combine all ingredients in small bowl. Mix thoroughly. Set aside.

Batter: Combine all ingredients in mixing bowl. Mix thoroughly. Set aside.

Preheat oven to 350°.

French Toast Stuffing: Heat butter in sauté pan. Add sugar and water and cook until sugar begins to caramelize. Add bananas, stirring to thoroughly coat. Add peaches and continue cooking until bananas and peaches are carmelized, approximately 6 to 8 minutes. Cool.

Lay piece of bread flat on cutting board. Beginning on the right side, slice bread through horizontally from right to left leaving ½″ uncut on left side.

Carefully fill each piece of bread with ¼ cup of the French Toast Stuffing. Gently lay bread in batter. Allow to rest for 1 minute. Carefully turn bread to other side and allow to sit for one additional minute in batter.

Transfer bread to sauté pan and cook on both sides on medium heat until golden, approximately 2 to 3 minutes on each side.

Sprinkle each piece of toast with 2 tablespoons of Streusel Topping and place in oven for 6 to 8 minutes or until topping browns.

Sprinkle with powdered sugar and serve with maple syrup.

Apple Praline French Toast

12 slices cinnamon raisin bread

2 tablespoons powdered sugar, for garnish

maple syrup

Apple Praline Topping

3 tablespoons butter, softened

1½ cups Granny Smith apples, chopped into ½″ pieces

⅓ cup chopped pecans

⅓ cup brown sugar

⅓ cup hot water

Batter

4 eggs

2 cups milk

2 tablespoons Cointreau® liqueur, optional

2 teaspoons vanilla extract

¼ teaspoon ground cinnamon

Apple Praline Topping: Melt butter in medium sauté pan. Add apples and cook for 5 minutes. Add pecans and cook for 5 additional minutes. Mix in brown sugar and water and cook, stirring constantly, until sauce thickens, about 5 minutes.

Batter: Combine all ingredients in medium bowl.

Soak sliced bread in batter mix for 5 minutes, turning after 2½ minutes. Place soaked bread on hot griddle and cook on both sides until golden, approximately 3 to 4 minutes.

Transfer toast to serving plate and ladle Apple Praline Topping over the toast. Sprinkle with powdered sugar. Serve with maple syrup.

Apple Maple Waffles

2	Granny Smith apples, peeled & thinly sliced
1½	cups all-purpose flour
¼	cup maple syrup
1	tablespoon baking powder
½	teaspoon baking soda
½	teaspoon salt
½	teaspoon cinnamon
½	teaspoon nutmeg
3	eggs, separated
2	tablespoons butter, melted
1	cup + 4 tablespoons buttermilk
¼	cup apple cider

Apple Praline Topping

3	tablespoons butter, softened
1½	cups Granny Smith apples, diced into ½″ pieces
⅔	cup pecans, chopped
⅓	cup brown sugar
⅓	cup hot water

To prepare waffles: Place sliced apples in boiling water and poach until tender, approximately 10 minutes. Set aside.

In medium bowl, blend dry ingredients together. Set aside.

In large bowl, beat together egg yolks, butter, buttermilk, and apple cider. Stir in cooked apples. Add dry ingredients, mix well.

In separate bowl beat egg whites until soft peaks are formed. Fold into batter mixture.

Pour 1 cup of batter (for each waffle) into hot waffle iron and cook until golden.

Top each waffle with Apple Praline Topping. Sprinkle with powdered sugar. Serve with maple syrup.

Apple Praline Topping: Melt butter in medium sauté pan. Add apples and cook for 5 minutes. Add pecans and cook for an additional 5 minutes. Stir in brown sugar and water; cook, stirring constantly, until sauce thickens, approximately 5 minutes.

Albuquerque Eggs Benedict

1 cup Black Bean Salsa
8 poached eggs
8 spicy sausage patties
2 flour tortillas, cut into strips & fried
4 teaspoons chopped parsley, for garnish
  fresh fruit, for garnish

Cilantro Cream

2 tablespoons sour cream
1 tablespoon heavy cream
1 teaspoon cilantro, finely chopped
⅛ teaspoon salt
  pinch white pepper
1 teaspoon hot sauce

Fresh Tomato Salsa

3 plum tomatoes, seeded and chopped
  into small pieces
1 teaspoon cilantro, finely chopped
½ jalapeño pepper, seeded and finely
  chopped
½ small red onion, finely chopped
1 clove garlic, finely chopped
½ teaspoon fresh lime juice
¼ teaspoon salt
  pinch ground black pepper

Black Bean Salsa

¼ lb. black beans
¼ cup red onion, chopped into ½″
  pieces
1 tablespoon cilantro, finely chopped
1 tablespoon lime juice
1 tablespoon olive oil
½ teaspoon salt
  pinch black pepper

Cook sausage patties in large sauté pan until cooked thoroughly, approximately 10 minutes.

Arrange tortilla strips in center of plate. Place two sausage patties on tortilla strips. Place a poached egg on each sausage. Spoon ¼ cup Tomato Salsa and Black Bean Salsa around sausage and egg. Drizzle with approximately 2 teaspoons of Cilantro Cream.

Garnish with parsley and fresh fruit.

Cilantro Cream: Combine creams, cilantro, salt, pepper, and hot sauce in bowl. Set aside.

Fresh Tomato Salsa: Place all ingredients in a medium bowl; mix well. Refrigerate.

Black Bean Salsa: Soak beans in water overnight. Drain. In a large saucepan, slowly cook beans in simmering water until tender, approximately 1 hour.

Place all ingredients in bowl and mix thoroughly.

Mix Tomato Salsa and Black Bean Salsa together. Set aside.

Masa Corncakes with Poached Eggs

8   Masa Corncakes
8   poached eggs
     Chipotle Salsa
1   cup Chorizo sausage, cooked &
        crumbled
4   tablespoons Jalapeño Cream
4   tablespoons green onion, chopped

Masa Corncake Mix

⅔   cup Masa flour
½   cup flour
½   cup yellow cornmeal
1   teaspoon sugar
1   teaspoon salt
1   teaspoon baking powder
1   teaspoon baking soda
2½   cups buttermilk
2   eggs
3   tablespoons Wesson® oil

Chipotle Salsa

1½   tablespoons olive oil
½   cup red onion, sliced thin
2   cloves garlic, minced
1½   cups tomatoes, chopped
1   jalapeño pepper, chopped
1   chipotle pepper, chopped
1   tablespoon cilantro, chopped
⅓   cup Black Bean Salsa

Masa Corncake Mix: Preheat oven to 350°.

Bake Masa flour oven for 10 minutes. Remove from oven. Sift Masa flour, flour, cornmeal, sugar, salt, baking powder, and baking soda into a large bowl.

In a separate bowl, whisk together buttermilk, eggs, and oil. Add to dry ingredients and stir until blended. Set aside until ready to serve.

Chipotle Salsa: Heat olive oil in sauté pan. Add onion and garlic and cook until softened. Mix in tomatoes, jalapeño and chipotle peppers. Bring to a boil. Once boiling, reduce heat to a simmer and continue cooking for an additional 10 minutes.

Remove 1 cup of the mixture from sauté pan and purée. Return puréed mixture to sauté pan. Stir in cilantro. Add Black Bean Salsa and mix well. Keep warm until ready to serve.

Black Bean Salsa: Soak black beans in water overnight. Drain. Slowly cook beans in a saucepan of simmering water until tender, approximately 1 hour.

Place all ingredients in bowl and mix thoroughly.

Jalapeño Cream: Whip heavy cream until it forms soft peaks. Add all other ingredients and purée in food processor until smooth. Store at room temperature.

To prepare Masa Corncakes: Ladle ¼ cup Masa Corncake mixture for each corncake onto hot griddle and cook until golden on both sides.

Place two corncakes side by side on each serving plate. Top each corncake with a poached egg. Ladle ¼ cup Chipotle and Black Bean Salsa down the center of the plate, between the two corncakes. Sprinkle 4 tablespoons of the cooked Chorizo sausage around the corncakes. Drizzle with Jalapeño Cream and garnish with chopped green onion.

Black Bean Salsa

¼ lb. black beans, soaked overnight & slowly cooked until tender, about 1 hour

¼ cup red onion, chopped into ½″ pieces

1 tablespoon cilantro, finely chopped

1 tablespoon lime juice

1 tablespoon olive oil

½ teaspoon salt

pinch black pepper

Jalapeño Cream

2 tablespoons heavy cream

2 teaspoons sour cream

½ jalapeño pepper, seeded & finely chopped

2 teaspoons cilantro, finely chopped

pinch white pepper

squeeze of lemon juice

Buttermilk Pancakes with Blueberry Compote

see photo SERVES **4**

106

16 Buttermilk Pancakes
1 cup Blueberry Compote
4 tablespoons Lemon Whipped Cream
  pure maple syrup

Buttermilk Pancake Mix

1¼ cups flour
2 tablespoons sugar
1 teaspoon baking powder
1 teaspoon baking soda
½ teaspoon salt
1½ cups buttermilk
1 cup crème fraîche or sour cream
1 egg
2 teaspoons vanilla extract

Blueberry Compote

1 cup blueberries
¼ cup sugar
¼ cup water

Lemon Whipped Cream

4 tablespoons heavy cream
¼ teaspoon lemon juice
1 tablespoon Cinnamon Crème Anglaise

Cinnamon Crème Anglaise

1 egg yolk
1 tablespoon + 1 teaspoon sugar
⅓ cup heavy cream
  pinch cinnamon
  dash of vanilla

Buttermilk Pancake Mix: Combine flour, sugar, baking powder, baking soda, and salt in a large bowl; mix thoroughly.

In a separate bowl, whisk buttermilk, crème fraîche, eggs and vanilla. Add to dry ingredients and stir until blended. Set aside until ready to serve.

Blueberry Compote: In a small saucepan, combine ½ cup of the blueberries with the sugar and water. Simmer over low heat until berries burst, approximately 5 minutes. Add remaining berries. Continue cooking until mixture covers the back of a wooden spoon, approximately 3 to 4 minutes.

Lemon Whipped Cream: In a medium bowl, beat cream until stiff. Add lemon juice and Cinnamon Crème Anglaise and mix thoroughly.

Cinnamon Crème Anglaise: In a small bowl, whisk together egg yolk and sugar until pale in color. Set aside.

In a medium saucepan, while stirring constantly, bring cream, cinnamon, and vanilla to a boil. Remove from heat.

Pour ¼ of the hot cream mixture into the egg yolk mixture; mix well. Transfer the entire yolk mixture into the saucepan containing the hot cream mixture. Cook over medium heat until sauce thickens and coats the back of a wooden spoon. Remove from heat.

Strain into clean bowl, stirring until cool.

To prepare Buttermilk Pancakes: For each pancake, pour ¼ cup of the Buttermilk Pancake Mix onto a hot griddle. Cook until golden on both sides.

Place 4 pancakes on a serving plate and ladle Blueberry Compote over pancake. Top with Lemon Whipped Cream. Serve with warm pure maple syrup.

The Lemon Whipped Cream is an excellent complement to the Blueberry Compote. Pure maple syrup will enhance this delicious breakfast.

Sunday Brunch Potato Hash Browns

1½ lbs. Yukon Gold potatoes, unpeeled,
      diced into ½″ pieces
¼   lb. bacon, cut into ½″ pieces
1   red bell pepper, finely chopped
1   yellow bell pepper, finely chopped
1   green bell pepper, finely chopped
¼   cup red onion, finely chopped
2   tablespoons Red Bell Pepper Butter
      (see page 22)
1   teaspoon kosher salt
⅓   teaspoon seasoning salt
¼   teaspoon black pepper

Steam potatoes until approximately ¾ done; cool.

Cook bacon in large sauté pan until crispy. Add potatoes and cook until golden brown. Stir in peppers and onion and continue cooking for another 2 to 3 minutes. Add Red Bell Pepper Butter and seasonings. Serve hot.

These are great potatoes to serve at any brunch.

Iowa City Steak Hash with Fried Eggs

¼ cup Red Bell Pepper Butter, (see page 22)

¼ cup olive oil

½ red bell pepper, chopped into ¼″ pieces

½ yellow bell pepper, chopped into ¼″ pieces

½ green bell pepper, chopped into ¼″ pieces

1 small red onion, chopped into ¼″ pieces

½ lb. Yukon Gold potatoes, unpeeled, diced into small pieces

1 lb. grilled marinated steak

1 teaspoon seasoning salt

½ teaspoon black pepper

1 teaspoon hot sauce

1 teaspoon chives, chopped, for garnish

6 eggs, large

Steak Marinade

2 jalapeño peppers, julienned & seeded

¼ small red onion, julienned

2 garlic cloves, minced

4 tablespoons fresh lime juice

8 sprigs cilantro

¼ cup olive oil

Steam potatoes until approximately ¾ done; cool.

To prepare hash: Heat oil and Red Bell Pepper Butter in sauté pan until hot. Add peppers, onion and potatoes and cook until tender, approximately 4 to 5 minutes. Mix in steak, seasoning salt, pepper, and hot sauce. Remove from heat; cool.

To serve, heat 2 tablespoons butter in sauté pan. Add 1 cup of hash and cook until golden, approximately 4 to 5 minutes.

Place on serving plate and top with fried eggs or any style egg you want. Top with chopped chives.

Steak Marinade: Combine all ingredients and mix well. Pour over steak and marinate in refrigerator for 1 hour. Grill steak until done to personal taste. Slice into small pieces.

Brunch

109

Smoked Chicken Hash

¼ cup butter

1 clove garlic, minced

1 small onion, chopped into ¼″ pieces

1 green onion, finely chopped

¼ red bell pepper, finely chopped

¼ yellow pepper, finely chopped

1 teaspoon salt

¼ teaspoon cayenne pepper

¼ teaspoon white pepper

2 teaspoons Worcestershire sauce

½ lb. Yukon Gold potatoes, boiled & diced into ¼″ pieces

1 lb. smoked chicken, diced into ½″ pieces

2 teaspoons fresh chives, chopped

6 eggs, large

Melt butter in large sauté pan. Add garlic and sauté for 1 minute. Add onions, yellow and red peppers and sauté until translucent. Mix in salt & peppers and Worcestershire sauce and cook for 2 minutes. Gently stir in diced potatoes. Add chicken and 1 teaspoon chives, (reserve remaining chives for garnish). Refrigerate until ready to use.

Heat 1 tablespoon butter in sauté pan. Add 1 cup of hash to sauté pan and gently pat to an oblong shape. Cook until golden brown, approximately 5 minutes on each side. Transfer hash to serving plate, top with poached egg.

Sprinkle with chopped chives. Serve with fresh fruit and toast and jam.

Meat & Poultry

THE RECIPES IN THIS CHAPTER REFLECT MY MIDWESTERN ROOTS.
TAKE A LITTLE TIME TO PREPARE THESE AND THE REWARDS WILL BE
GREAT. I REALLY LIKE THE DUCK WITH THE BLACKBERRY PORT
GLAZE. THE PORK TENDERLOIN IS MY MOTHER'S FAVORITE DISH.

Herb & Garlic Chicken Breast
with Spicy Apple Chutney

4   8 oz. chicken breasts

Herb Marinade

1   cup olive oil
1   tablespoon fresh rosemary, finely
     chopped
1   tablespoon fresh oregano, finely
     chopped
1   tablespoon fresh basil, finely chopped
     juice of 1 lemon
2   cloves garlic, minced
1   teaspoon salt
1   teaspoon black pepper

Spicy Apple Chutney

1   tablespoon vegetable oil
¼   very small red onion, diced into ¼″
     pieces
¼   red bell pepper, diced fine
¼   teaspoon dry mustard
½   teaspoon salt
1   clove garlic, minced
½   jalapeño pepper, minced
1   lb. Granny Smith apples, peeled &
     sliced thin
⅛   teaspoon ground allspice
⅛   teaspoon ground ginger
1   tablespoon golden raisins
3   tablespoons brown sugar
2   tablespoons red wine vinegar

To make marinade: Combine garlic and ½ cup olive oil in blender or food processor and purée garlic well. Transfer garlic mixture into medium bowl with all remaining ingredients and mix well. Let stand for one hour before using as marinade.

To prepare chicken: Place chicken breasts in ovenproof baking dish and pour marinade over chicken. Marinate in refrigerator for 24 hours prior to preparing chicken for serving.

Preheat oven to 450°.

Roast chicken in oven for 25-30 minutes or until skin is golden brown.

Place warm Apple Chutney on a serving plate and place chicken on top of chutney. Serve with Wild Rice Vegetable Blend or other desired side dish. Garnish with fresh herb sprigs.

Spicy Apple Chutney: Heat vegetable oil in sauté pan. Add red onion, red pepper, mustard, and salt; cook until translucent, approximately 5 minutes. Add garlic, jalapeño pepper, apples, allspice, and ginger; continue cooking for one minute. Add raisins, brown sugar, and vinegar and bring to a boil. Refrigerate until ready to use.

Honey Pecan Turkey Breast with
Sweet Potato-Parsnip Hash Browns

1½ lbs. fresh turkey breast, cut in ½″ slices
     flour for dusting
½ cup vegetable oil
     Honey Pecan Butter
4 teaspoons parsley, chopped

Honey Pecan Butter

½ cup butter
4 tablespoons honey
4 tablespoons pecans, chopped

Sweet Potato-Parsnip Hash Browns

1 lb. sweet potatoes, peeled & diced
     into ½″ pieces
¼ lb. parsnips, peeled & diced into ½″
     pieces
4 strips bacon
⅓ cup peanut oil
1 large red onion, finely chopped
1 teaspoon salt
¼ teaspoon black pepper
1 teaspoon parsley, chopped

Sautéed vegetables

2 tablespoons olive oil
1 cup zucchini, sliced thin
1 cup yellow squash, sliced thin
½ cup red onion, sliced thin

Dust turkey with flour. Heat vegetable oil in large sauté pan. Add turkey and cook until golden on both sides, approximately 8 to 10 minutes.

To serve: Place Sweet Potato-Parsnip Hash Browns in center of serving plate. Arrange turkey slices around hash browns and brush with Honey Pecan Butter. Garnish with sautéed vegetables. Sprinkle with chopped parsley.

Honey Pecan Butter: Melt butter in sauté pan. Blend in honey and bring to a boil.

Add pecans and mix thoroughly; continue cooking until a glaze forms, approximately 8-10 minutes.

Sweet Potato-Parsnip Hash Browns: Boil sweet potatoes until tender. Rinse with cold water. Set aside.

Boil parsnips until tender. Rinse with cold water. Set aside.

In medium sauté pan cook bacon until crispy. Drain grease. Add peanut oil and heat. Add red onion and cook until soft, approximately 4 minutes. Gently stir in potatoes and parsnips and cook until golden, approximately 5 minutes. Add salt, pepper, and parsley; mix thoroughly and remove from heat.

Sautéed vegetables: Heat olive oil in sauté pan. Add vegetables; sauté until tender, approximately 3 to 4 minutes. Remove from heat. Serve warm.

Beringer North Coast Zinfandel

Grilled Veal Flank Steak with Wild Mushrooms au Gratin

4 8 oz. pieces veal flank steak
Herb Marinade
4 Potato Leek Cakes (see recipe, page 163)

Herb Marinade

2 cloves garlic, minced
1 cup olive oil
1 tablespoon fresh rosemary
1 tablespoon fresh oregano
1 tablespoon fresh basil
1 lemon, sliced
2 teaspoons salt
1 teaspoon black pepper

Wild Mushroom au Gratin

¼ cup butter, melted
½ cup crimini mushrooms, sliced into ¼″ pieces
¼ cup oyster mushrooms, sliced into ½″ pieces
¼ cup shitake mushrooms, stems removed & sliced into ⅛″ pieces
¼ cup Parmesan cheese, grated
1 cup Egg/Cream Mixture

Egg/Cream Mixture

1 egg yolk
1 cup heavy cream.

Marinate veal in Herb Marinade for 24 hours in refrigerator. Grill veal until cooked to desired doneness. Slice on bias in ¼″ slices. Place on a serving plate and pour Wild Mushroom Au Gratin evenly over sliced veal. Serve with Potato Leek Cake and vegetable of choice.

Herb Marinade: Combine garlic and ½ cup olive oil in blender or food processor and process thoroughly. Transfer garlic mixture to medium bowl and add all remaining ingredients; mix well. Let stand for one hour before using as marinade.

Wild Mushroom au Gratin: Heat butter in sauté pan. Add mushrooms and sauté for 4 to 5 minutes, until mushrooms are tender.

Stir in Parmesan cheese and Egg/Cream Mixture. Continue cooking until sauce begins to thicken. Remove from heat and serve immediately.

Egg/Cream Mixture: Blend together.

Fleur De Carneros Pinot Noir

Grilled Sirloin with Peppercorn Butter and Merlot Sauce

4   12 oz. N.Y. steaks, trimmed
     Peppercorn Butter
     Merlot Sauce
4   Potato Leek Cakes (see recipe, page 163)
1   lb. Roasted Asparagus

Peppercorn Butter

½   cup merlot wine
1   shallot, thinly sliced
1½   teaspoons balsamic vinegar
1   sprig fresh thyme
1   sprig fresh rosemary
     pinch dry mustard
4   tablespoons butter, softened
     pinch cracked peppercorn blend
¼   teaspoon Dijon mustard
     pinch kosher salt

Merlot Sauce

4   tablespoons butter, softened
2   tablespoons cornstarch
¼   cup olive oil
6   cloves garlic, minced
⅓   cup red wine vinegar
3   cups merlot wine
4   cups Brown Chicken Stock (see
       page 23)
2   tablespoons fresh thyme, finely
       chopped

Grill or broil steaks to personal taste.

Place steaks on a serving plate. Pour ¼ cup Merlot Sauce over each steak, put 1 tablespoon Peppercorn Butter on top of steak and serve with Potato Leek Cake and Roasted Asparagus.

Roasted Asparagus: Trim ends of asparagus, and coat with ¼ cup olive oil, 1 tablespoon kosher salt, and 1 teaspoon black pepper. Roast in 400° oven for 15 minutes until cooked.

Peppercorn Butter: Combine merlot, shallot, vinegar, fresh herbs, and dry mustard in a medium saucepan. Boil over medium heat until liquid is syrupy, approximately 15 to 20 minutes. Remove herb sprigs and cool.

Add butter, cracked peppercorn blend, Dijon mustard and salt to cooled butter mixture; blend thoroughly. Refrigerate until ready to serve.

Merlot Sauce: Mix softened butter and cornstarch together to form a paste. Set aside.

Heat oil in large saucepan. Add garlic and sauté for 30 seconds. Add red wine vinegar and merlot; heat sauce to just under a boil; continue cooking until liquid is reduced by ¾, approximately 15 to 20 minutes. Add Chicken Stock; return to just under a boil and continue cooking until liquid is reduced again by ¾. Strain, returning sauce to saucepan.

Stir in butter/cornstarch paste and whisk until thoroughly blended. Add fresh thyme and cook for 5 minutes or until sauce begins to thicken. Cool.

Meat & Poultry

117

Ferrari-Carano Merlot

Pork Tenderloin with Dried Cherry Compote

6   6 oz. pieces pork tenderloin
    Mustard Marinade
6   sprigs fresh rosemary, for garnish
    Dried Cherry Compote
    Corn Pudding

Mustard Marinade

1   cup olive oil
2   cloves garlic
⅓   cup Dijon mustard
2   teaspoons black pepper
1   teaspoon kosher salt
2   teaspoons thyme, finely chopped
1   teaspoon rosemary, finely chopped

Dried Cherry Compote

½   small red onion, diced
¼   cup shitake mushrooms
1   tablespoon olive oil
3   cups Beef Stock (see page 24)
1   teaspoon orange zest
2   cups Cabernet Sauvignon wine
1   cup dried cherries
¼   cup orange juice
1   tablespoon thyme, chopped
½   cup port wine
3   tablespoons butter, chilled, cut into
        pieces

Corn Pudding

6   ears fresh corn
1   cup heavy cream
3   eggs

Mustard Marinade: In a blender, purée olive oil and garlic. Add remaining ingredients and blend well.

Marinate pork tenderloin in Mustard Marinade in refrigerator for a minimum of 4 hours. Grill or broil tenderloin until medium, approximately 8 to 10 minutes. Slice on bias into ¼″ pieces. Place Corn Pudding in middle of serving plate, ladle ¼ cup Cherry Compote on plate and place sliced pork on top of compote. Garnish with fresh rosemary sprigs.

Dried Cherry Compote: Sauté red onions and shitake mushrooms in olive oil until lightly browned, approximately 3 to 5 minutes. Add Beef Stock, orange zest, Cabernet Sauvignon; bring to a boil and continue cooking until liquid is reduced by half. Add dried cherries, orange juice, thyme, and port wine. Return to a boil and continue cooking until liquid is of a syrupy consistency. Remove from heat and whisk in chilled butter, one piece at a time. Return to a boil prior to serving.

Corn Pudding: Preheat oven to 300°.

Slice corn from the cob and place into medium bowl.

Purée approximately ⅔ of corn with cream, eggs, sugar, and salt. Return puréed corn mixture to bowl of whole corn. Add remaining ingredients and mix well.

Grease six - 6 oz. ramekins or soufflé dishes. Fill each with approximately ½ cup Corn Pudding. Place in an ovenproof pan filled halfway with water. Bake for 60 minutes or until pudding is set.

David Bruce Pinot Noir - Sonoma County

2   tablespoons sugar
1   teaspoon salt
1½ tablespoons flour
1   teaspoon baking powder
¼   cup butter, melted
1   tablespoon parsley, chopped
1   tablespoon Parmesan cheese, grated
     pinch allspice
     pinch cayenne pepper

Braised Lamb Shanks with Red Pepper Polenta and Tuscan Beans

6 12 to14 oz. lamb shanks
¾ cup kosher salt
1 cup olive oil
   Lamb jus
   Red Pepper Polenta
   Tuscan Beans
   Lemon Gremalata

Lamb jus

1 cup olive oil
1 lb. Spanish onions, sliced
2 small carrots, chopped
2 celery ribs, chopped
1 cup red wine
6 garlic cloves, crushed
2 teaspoons black peppercorns
3 cups Chicken Stock (see page 23)
2 cups Beef Stock (see page 24)
1 tablespoon basil, chopped
2 teaspoons rosemary, chopped

Tuscan Beans

1 tablespoon extra virgin olive oil
¼ cup pancetta, sliced into small pieces
½ lb. Cannellini beans, soaked overnight
1 sprig rosemary
1 sprig oregano
2 cloves garlic, minced
½ cup tomatoes, diced
¼ cup dry white wine
2 cups Chicken Broth
2 teaspoons kosher salt
½ teaspoon black pepper

Preheat oven to 300°.

Sprinkle salt over lamb shanks. Heat olive oil in large sauté pan; add lamb shanks and brown on all sides, approximately 8-10 minutes. Set aside.

Lamb jus: Add olive oil to large ovenproof roasting pan and brown onions, carrots, and celery until golden, approximately 10 minutes. Stir in red wine, bring to a boil and continue cooking until liquid is reduced by ½, approximately 20 minutes.

Add garlic, black pepper, Chicken Stock, Beef Stock, basil, rosemary, and the browned lamb shanks. Cover and bake in oven for 3 hours, or until lamb shanks are tender.

Remove lamb shanks from pan and keep warm.

Strain jus from roasting pan into saucepan. Heat to boiling and continue cooking until liquid is reduced by half.

To serve: Place approximately ½ cup Red Pepper Polenta in center of each plate. Place one lamb shank on polenta, spoon Tuscan Beans over lamb and polenta. Ladle hot lamb jus over all. Garnish with Lemon Gremalata.

Tuscan Beans: Heat olive oil in saucepan. Add pancetta and cook until crispy. Add remaining ingredients, cover and cook for 25 minutes. Transfer to 300° oven and bake for 2 hours. Check to see if additional liquid is needed, if so, add a little more chicken broth and bake for one additional hour or until beans are soft.

Lemon Gremalata: Combine all ingredients; mix well.

Red Pepper Polenta: Preheat oven to 350°.

In an ovenproof pan, bring water, vegetable stock, and garlic to a boil. Stir in cornmeal, grits, and red pepper, reduce heat and continue cooking for 5 minutes, stirring constantly.

Lemon Gremalata

1 clove garlic, minced
 zest of 1 lemon
1 sprig parsley, finely chopped

Red Pepper Polenta

1½ cups water
4 cups vegetable stock
1 tablespoon garlic, minced
⅔ cup yellow cornmeal
⅔ cup grits
1 small red pepper, roasted & puréed
1 cup sour cream
¼ cup Monterey Jack cheese, shredded
¼ cup Parmesan cheese, grated
4 tablespoons butter
1 teaspoon salt
¼ teaspoon white pepper

Cover and place in oven for 30 minutes.

Remove from oven. Stir in sour cream, cheeses, salt, and white pepper; mix thoroughly.

Red Pepper Polenta can be kept warm in a covered pan set over a double boiler.

Braised Beef Short Ribs with Gorgonzola Polenta Cakes

12	10 oz. beef short ribs
8	tablespoons kosher salt
1	cup olive oil
1	lb. Spanish onions, sliced
¼	lb. celery, chopped
½	lb. carrots, peeled & sliced
1	cup red wine
6	cloves garlic, smashed
2	teaspoons black peppercorns
6	cups Beef Stock (see page 24)
4	sprigs fresh basil, chopped
2	teaspoons fresh rosemary, chopped
12	baby carrots, peeled, blanched, & trimmed
12	parsnips, peeled, blanched, & cut on bias
12	turnips, peeled, blanched, & cut into wedges
6	3″ Gorgonzola Polenta Cakes
¾	cup shallots, carmelized
6	teaspoons parsley, chopped

Gorgonzola Polenta Cakes

2	cups water
2	cups vegetable broth
1	teaspoon garlic, minced
1	cup yellow cornmeal
⅔	cup sour cream
¼	cup Parmesan cheese, grated
¼	cup Gorgonzola cheese, crumbled
3	tablespoons butter
½	teaspoon kosher salt
¼	teaspoon white pepper

Preheat oven to 300°.

Trim two of the bones off each short rib beginning at the skinniest tip. Trim excess fat. Fold meat around remaining bone and tie with butcher string. Sprinkle with salt.

Heat ½ cup olive oil in large roasting pan. Brown short ribs; remove from pan and set aside.

Add remaining olive oil to pan and heat. Add onions, celery and carrots; sauté until brown, approximately 6-8 minutes. Add red wine; bring to a boil and continue cooking until liquid is reduced by half.

Add garlic, black pepper, Beef Stock, basil, rosemary, and short ribs. Cover pan and roast in oven for 3 hours, or until tender. Remove short ribs, and keep warm.

Strain jus from roasting pan; return to stove and boil until liquid is reduced by half.

Preheat oven to 400°.

Place short ribs, baby carrots, parsnips, and turnips in covered baking pan. Pour jus over all. Bake in oven for 20 minutes.

Place Gorgonzola Polenta Cakes in center of platter. Arrange short ribs around polenta. Ladle vegetables on platter. Pour jus over all. Garnish with carmelized shallots and chopped parsley.

Gorgonzola Polenta Cakes: Preheat oven to 350°.

In a medium ovenproof pan, bring water, vegetable broth, and garlic to a boil. Stir in cornmeal, reduce heat and cook for 5 minutes, stirring constantly.

Cover pan and place in oven. Bake for 30 minutes.

Remove from oven and stir in sour cream, cheeses, butter, salt, and pepper.

Columbia Crest Merlot - Washington

Carmelized Shallots

1	tablespoon olive oil
1	tablespoon butter
½	cup shallots, whole, peeled

Pour onto greased 11x13″ baking dish and cool. Allow to set. Cut Polenta into 2x2″ squares. Place under broiler and cook until golden brown, about 3-4 minutes.

Carmelized Shallots: Heat olive oil and butter in a sauté pan. Add shallots and cook over medium heat until shallots are golden in color, approximately 10-15 minutes.

Grilled Ribeye with Gorgonzola Sauce

4   10 oz. ribeye steaks
     Ribeye Marinade
     Gorgonzola Sauce
4   tablespoons Gorgonzola cheese,
     grated
4   fresh herb sprigs, such as rosemary
     or thyme

Ribeye Marinade

1   cup olive oil
2   tablespoons dry mustard
1   tablespoon Worcestershire sauce
1   teaspoon garlic, minced
1   teaspoon soy sauce
1   teaspoon lemon juice
⅛   teaspoon hot sauce
¼   teaspoon kosher salt
⅛   teaspoon cracked black pepper

Gorgonzola Sauce

¼   cup butter for sautéing onion
¼   cup butter cut into pieces & chilled
½   small red onion, finely chopped
1½ cups Madeira sherry
3   cups Beef Stock (see page 24)
1   cup Gorgonzola cheese, crumbled

Marinate steaks in Ribeye Marinade for 4 hours in refrigerator.

Grill steak to personal taste. Ladle Gorgonzola Sauce over steaks and sprinkle with grated Gorgonzola cheese. Garnish with fresh herb sprigs.

Ribeye Marinade: Combine all ingredients; mix well.

Gorgonzola Sauce: Melt ¼ cup butter in sauté pan. Add onion and sauté until brown. Add Madeira, bring to a boil and continue cooking until liquid is reduced by half, approximately 15 to 20 minutes.

Add Beef Stock; return to a boil and continue cooking until liquid is reduced by half again.

Slowly add chilled butter pieces, whisking to dissolve.

Add cheese and mix well. Remove from heat.

Firestone Merlot – Santa Ynez Valley   *Serve with Redskin Mashers, page 164.*

Grilled Lamb Chops with Orzo Pasta and Mint Aioli

16 lamb chops, 1″ thick
    Lamb Marinade
    Orzo, Radicchio, & Pancetta
16 pieces asparagus, grilled
8   tablespoons Mint Aioli (see page 36)
4   sprigs fresh herbs, (mint, rosemary,
        oregano, or thyme)

Lamb Marinade

1   cup olive oil
2   cloves garlic, chopped fine
1   tablespoon fresh rosemary, finely
        chopped
1   tablespoon fresh basil, finely chopped
1   tablespoon fresh oregano, finely
        chopped
1   teaspoon kosher salt
¼   teaspoon cracked black pepper

Orzo, Radicchio, & Pancetta

¼   cup pancetta, julienned thin
1   cup orzo pasta, cooked
¼   cup Olive Oil, Garlic & Herb Sauce
        (see page 18)
½   cup radicchio, thinly sliced
4   pieces sun dried tomatoes, julienned
12 Calamata olives, quartered

Prepare Lamb Marinade; marinate lamb chops for 24 hours.

Prepare Orzo, Radicchio, & Pancetta. Set aside.

Preheat grill or broiler.

Grill lamb chops to personal taste.

Grill asparagus.

To serve: Place Orzo, Radicchio, & Pancetta in the center of each plate. Top with grilled asparagus; arrange lamb chops around orzo; drizzle with Mint Aioli. Garnish with fresh herb sprigs.

Lamb Marinade: Combine all ingredients; blend thoroughly.

Orzo, Radicchio, & Pancetta: In medium sauté pan, cook pancetta until crispy. Drain. Stir in cooked orzo and Olive Oil, Garlic & Herb Sauce; mix well.

Add remaining ingredients and toss to coat. Keep warm until ready to serve.

Fife Redhead Zinfandel

Oven Roasted Duck with Blackberry Port Glaze

see photo SERVES **4**

2 fresh 4 to 5 lb. Long Island ducks
Duck Seasoning
Blackberry Port Glaze
Fresh herb sprigs for garnish

Duck Seasoning
½ teaspoon thyme
½ teaspoon rosemary
1 teaspoon cracked black pepper
1 teaspoon kosher salt
1 tablespoon garlic, minced

Blackberry Port Glaze
1 cup port wine
⅔ cup blackberries
¼ red onion, finely chopped
¼ teaspoon cracked black pepper
⅓ cup Chicken Stock (see page 23)
⅓ cup Beef Stock (see page 24)
2 tablespoons butter, chilled
¼ teaspoon salt
⅛ teaspoon white pepper

Duck Seasoning: Combine all ingredients in small bowl; mix well.

To prepare duck: Remove wrapper from duck, remove giblets and neck from inside duck cavity and discard. Place on metal baking sheet and air-dry in refrigerator for 24 hours.

Pierce skin with fork and rub Duck Seasoning both inside and on entire outside skin. Place in ovenproof pan and roast in 300° oven for 2 hours. Remove from oven and cool.

Cut ducks in half lengthwise from head to tail. Remove wing tips, breast bones, back bones, and thigh bones. Cut off leg tips. Cut duck in half by the breast and thigh. Ladle ¼ cup of Blackberry Port Glaze over duck and place in 400° oven for 10 minutes.

Ladle remaining Blackberry Port Glaze over each piece of duck and garnish with fresh herb sprigs.

Blackberry Port Glaze: In medium saucepan combine port, blackberries, red onion, and cracked black pepper. Bring to a boil and continue cooking until liquid is reduced by half. Add Chicken and Beef Stock; return to a boil and continue cooking until liquid is reduced by half again.

Remove from heat, pour into food processor and purée. Strain into serving bowl. Whisk in chilled butter one piece at a time. Season with salt and white pepper.

Meat & Poultry

127

Guenoc "Lodi" Zinfandel   *Serve with Dried Fruit Couscous, page 170.*

Maple Cured Pork Loin with Whipped Sweet Potatoes

2   lbs. boneless pork loin
2   cups Maple Cured Pork Loin Marinade
4   cups Whipped Sweet Potatoes
4   sprigs fresh herbs, for garnish
    Red Onion Marmalade (see page 158)
    Grilled Maple Corn and Bacon Relish
      (see page 36)

Maple Cured Pork Loin Marinade

½   cup soy sauce
¼   cup dark beer
2   tablespoons dark molasses
2   teaspoons lemon zest
2   teaspoon orange zest
1   tablespoon fresh thyme, chopped fine
2   tablespoon ginger
2   cloves garlic, chopped fine
2   tablespoon brown sugar
½   teaspoon cracked black pepper
1   tablespoon kosher salt
½   teaspoon cayenne pepper

Whipped Sweet Potatoes

4   sweet potatoes, peeled, cut in 1″ pieces
1   Granny Smith apple, peeled, cored, and
      diced fine
½   cup heavy cream
¼   cup butter
2   teaspoon brown sugar
1   tablespoon maple syrup
1   teaspoon kosher salt
½   teaspoon black pepper

Place entire pork loin in baking dish, cover completely with marinade, refrigerate for 24 hours.

Remove from marinade and place in oven at 400° for 1 hour or until cooked to medium.

Slice pork loin and place on serving plate. Placed Whipped Sweet Potatoes in center next to pork. Place hot Grilled Maple Corn and Bacon Relish next to pork and drizzle warm Red Onion Marmalade over top of pork. Garnish with a fresh herb sprig.

Maple Cured Pork Loin Marinade: Combine all ingredients in a mixing bowl and mix well.

Whipped Sweet Potatoes: Put sweet potatoes in a large pot, cover with water and bring to a boil. Cook until tender.

In a saucepan combine apple, cream, butter, brown sugar, and maple syrup. Bring to a simmer.

Drain potatoes and transfer to mixer and whip with wisk. Gradually add cream mixture and whip. Add salt and pepper.

Dehlinger Goldridge Vineyard - Pinot Noir

Pastas & Pizzas

THE MOST IMPORTANT THING ABOUT COOKING PASTA IS COOKING IT AL DENTE AND SERVING IT WITH A GREAT SAUCE. I THINK WE DO A GOOD JOB OF THIS IN THE RESTAURANT. BEFORE ATTEMPTING ANY OF THE RECIPES IN THIS CHAPTER, FAMILIARIZE YOURSELF WITH THE SAUCES IN THE BASICS CHAPTER. THIS WILL MAKE THINGS MUCH EASIER.

Filling

⅓	cup olive oil
1	lb. chicken breast, cooked, chopped very fine
¼	lb. Italian sausage, cooked, chopped fine
¼	cup button mushrooms, sliced ¼″
¼	cup shitake mushrooms, sliced ¼″
1	clove garlic, minced
½	lb. spinach, chopped into 1″ pieces
1	tablespoon fresh oregano, finely chopped
2	teaspoons salt
1	teaspoon black pepper
½	lb. mozzarella cheese, shredded
½	lb. ricotta cheese
⅓	cup Romano cheese, grated
⅓	cup fresh basil, julienned ¼″

Cannelloni

16	4x6″ pasta sheets
	Tomato-Butter Sauce (see page 22)
1	lb. mozzarella cheese, grated, for topping
1	tablespoon fresh parsley, chopped

In large bowl combine chicken breasts and sausage. Set aside.

Heat olive oil in large sauté pan. Sauté mushrooms and garlic until mushrooms are softened, approximately 3 to 4 minutes. Add spinach and reduce heat, cook until liquid is evaporated, approximately 5 minutes. Add oregano, salt, and pepper, and mix well. Remove from heat. Combine with meat mixture. Cool.

Stir in cheeses and basil, mix well. Refrigerate until ready to use.

Preheat oven to 400°.

To assemble Cannelloni: To assemble: place ¼ cup of filling in center of each pasta sheet. Roll tightly. Place cannellonis in ovenproof pan. Ladle Tomato Butter Sauce over cannelloni. Sprinkle mozzarella cheese evenly over sauce. Bake in oven for 15-20 minutes or until heated through.

Spoon sauce from pan onto serving platter. Transfer cannelloni to top of sauce. Sprinkle with chopped parsley.

Rabbit Ridge Zinfandel – Amador County

Seafood Cannelloni

Filling

1	lb. shrimp, peeled, deveined
½	lb. lobster meat, cooked, chopped
½	lb. jumbo crabmeat
¼	lb. peppered smoked salmon (see page 202, *also available at most seafood markets*)
1	clove roasted garlic, minced (see page 25)
1	tablespoon fresh oregano, finely chopped
1	cup ricotta cheese
¼	cup cottage cheese
⅔	cup Parmesan cheese, shredded
½	cup mozzarella cheese, shredded
¼	cup fresh basil, julienned ¼″

Roasted Tomato Sauce

8	plum tomatoes, halved
2	tablespoons shallots
2	cloves garlic
2	tablespoons olive oil
	pinch black pepper
2	sprigs fresh thyme
2	sprigs fresh chives
2	sprigs fresh oregano
1	tablespoons balsamic vinegar
	pinch salt

Cannelloni

16	4x6 rectangular pasta sheets
	Roasted Tomato Sauce
1	cup Parmesan cheese, for topping
1	cup mozzarella cheese, for topping
4	tablespoons chives, chopped

In large bowl, combine shrimp, lobster, crabmeat, salmon, garlic, and oregano; mix well.

In a separate bowl, mix cheeses and basil. Combine with seafood mixture.

To assemble Cannelloni: Preheat oven to 400°.

To assemble: place ¼ cup of filling in the center of each pasta sheet. Roll tightly to form cannelloni. Ladle ½ cup of Roasted Tomato Sauce onto bottom of baking dish. Place cannellonis on top of sauce. Ladle with the rest of Roasted Tomato Sauce. Sprinkle evenly with Parmesan and mozzarella cheese.

Bake in 400° oven for 20 minutes, or until cheese is golden. Sprinkle a little extra Parmesan cheese on top of cannelloni. Sprinkle with chopped chives.

Roasted Tomato Sauce: Preheat oven to 450°.

Place tomatoes in heavy baking pan with shallots and garlic. Drizzle with olive oil. Sprinkle with black pepper and herbs. Bake in oven for 30 minutes or until tomatoes are well done.

Remove from oven and transfer to a food processor. Purée until well blended. Add balsamic vinegar and salt; purée until smooth.

Keep warm until ready to serve.

Truchard Pinot Noir

Roasted Vegetable Cannelloni

Cheese Mix

1	lb. ricotta cheese
¼	cup cottage cheese
⅔	cup fresh Parmesan cheese, grated
½	cup fresh basil, finely chopped
¼	cup Tomato-Basil Sauce (see page 18)
1	teaspoon salt
¼	teaspoon white pepper
2	tablespoons Basil Pesto (see page 21)

Roasted Vegetable Mix

2	tablespoons olive oil
¼	lb. shitake mushrooms, sliced into ½″ pieces
¼	lb. red onions, chopped fine
1	small carrot, blanched, chopped ¼″ pieces
1	small yellow squash, chopped ¼″ pieces
1	small zucchini, chopped ¼″ pieces
½	red bell pepper, chopped ¼″ pieces
½	yellow bell pepper, chopped ¼″ pieces
	salt to taste

Cannelloni

16	4x6 rectangular pasta sheets
	Cheese Mix
	Tomato-Basil Sauce
1	cup Parmesan cheese, for topping
1	cup mozzarella cheese, for topping
4	tablespoons chives, chopped

Cheese Mix: Thoroughly mix all ingredients in bowl. Refrigerate until ready to use.

Roasted Vegetable Mix: Preheat oven to 400°.

Brush vegetables with olive oil and place in ovenproof pan. Sprinkle with salt.

Bake in oven until soft, about 20 minutes. Refrigerate until ready to use.

Cannelloni: Preheat oven to 400°.

To assemble: Place ¼ cup Cheese Mix on each pasta sheet. Add ¼ cup Roasted Vegetable Mix. Roll tightly.

Place cannellonis in ovenproof pan. Ladle Tomato-Basil Sauce over cannelloni. Top with Parmesan and mozzarella cheese. Bake in oven for 20 minutes, or until cheese is golden brown. Remove from oven and sprinkle with chopped chives.

Pastas & Pizzas

Ravenswood Petite Sirah

Pan-Seared Salmon Pasta

4   6 oz. pieces salmon fillet
¼   cup olive oil
     Cajun spices for dusting
1   cup Olive Oil, Garlic & Herb Sauce
       (see page 18)
1   red pepper, julienned fine
1   yellow pepper, julienned fine
16   Calamata olives, pitted & halved
½   lb. French beans, trimmed
4   teaspoons fresh parsley, chopped
1   lb. penne pasta, cooked & drained
     Tomato Saffron Aioli

Tomato Saffron Aioli
1   egg yolk
1   tablespoon tomato, chopped
1   tablespoon fresh basil, chopped
¼   teaspoon garlic, minced
     pinch saffron
¼   cup olive oil
⅛   teaspoon salt
     pinch white pepper
2   teaspoons lemon juice

Heat olive oil in sauté pan. Brush salmon with olive oil; dust with Cajun spices. Place salmon in sauté pan and cook on both sides until salmon is cooked, about 8-10 minutes. Remove from pan, set aside and keep warm.

In the same sauté pan, heat Olive Oil, Garlic, & Herb Sauce. Add, red and yellow pepper, olives, and French beans, stirring continually until warm. Add cooked pasta and toss well.

Transfer cooked pasta and vegetables to large serving platter. Arrange salmon on top of pasta and vegetables. Drizzle with Tomato Saffron Aioli and sprinkle with chopped parsley.

Tomato Saffron Aioli: In food processor, combine egg yolk, tomato, basil, garlic, and saffron; process until blended. With machine running, slowly pour in olive oil and process until smooth.

Add salt, white pepper, and lemon juice; process until blended. Serve warm.

Toad Hollow Pinot Noir – Russian River

Smoked Chicken Breast with Pancetta & Angel Hair Pasta

½ lb. pancetta, sliced thin, julienned into ½″ pieces

4 tablespoons fresh basil, julienned into thin strips

1 teaspoon red pepper flakes

1 lb. smoked chicken breast (see page 202 or page 26) skin removed, cut into ¼″ slices

1 cup Tomato-Basil Sauce (see page 18)

1 cup Olive Oil, Garlic & Herb Sauce (see page 18)

1 lb. angel hair pasta, cooked al dente, drained

4 teaspoons parsley, chopped

In large sauté pan cook pancetta until crispy. Add basil and red pepper flakes; mix well. Stir in smoked chicken, Tomato-Basil Sauce, and Olive Oil, Garlic, & Herb Sauce. Heat thoroughly.

Toss in cooked angel hair pasta. Mix thoroughly.

Transfer to large serving platter. Sprinkle with chopped parsley.

Cain Cuvee

Pasta Jambalaya

½ cup Olive Oil, Garlic & Herb Sauce (see page 18)

½ cup Red Bell Pepper Butter (see page 22)

½ lb. chicken breast, grilled, julienned into ½″ strips

8 large shrimp, tails removed, peeled & deveined

½ lb. andouille sausage, chargrilled, sliced on bias into ¼″ slices

2 teaspoon Cajun spices

1 small red onion, julienned into ¼″ strips

¼ cup red pepper, julienned into ¼″ strips

¼ cup yellow pepper, julienned into ¼″ strips

¼ cup green pepper, julienned into ¼″ strips

¼ cup fresh spinach, steamed

16 cherry tomatoes

1 lb. fettuccine, cooked

Heat Olive Oil, Garlic, & Herb Sauce and Red Bell Pepper Butter in large sauté pan. Add all remaining ingredients, except fettuccine, and sauté until thoroughly heated, approximately 5 to 6 minutes.

Add fettuccine and toss well.

Pour onto serving platter.

Firestone Old Vines Zinfandel

New Bedford Littleneck Clam Linguine

24 littleneck clams
½ lb. Italian sausage, sliced into ¼″ pieces
2 jalapeño peppers, seeded, chopped fine
1 small red onion, julienned into thin strips
1 teaspoon red pepper flakes
1 cup Garlic Butter
1 cup chardonnay wine
1 cup Tomato-Basil Sauce (see page 18)
1 cup water
1 lb. linguine, cooked
4 teaspoons green onions, sliced thin

Garlic Butter

1 cup butter, softened
1 clove garlic, roasted (see page 25)
¼ cup dry white wine
2 teaspoons parsley, finely chopped
1 tablespoon roasted yellow pepper, diced
1 tablespoon roasted red pepper, diced
½ teaspoon kosher salt
¼ teaspoon cracked black pepper

Place all ingredients, except linguine, in large sauté pan, cover and cook until clams open, about 10 to 12 minutes. Discard any unopened clams.

Add linguine and toss well. Transfer to serving platter and top with sliced green onions.

Garlic Butter: Beat softened butter at medium speed with mixer until soft and fluffy. Set aside.

In food processor, blend garlic and wine until thoroughly mixed. Add remaining ingredients and softened butter; process until blended.

Pastas & Pizzas

Shafer Red Shoulder Ranch Chardonnay

Grilled Chicken Fettuccine

4   6 to 8 oz. skinless chicken breasts, halved

4   tablespoons olive oil

1½ cups Red Bell Pepper Butter (see page 22)

½   cup Tomato-Basil Sauce (see page 18)

½   cup Olive Oil, Garlic & Herb Sauce (see page 18)

¼   cup button mushrooms, sliced ¼″

16 pieces asparagus, blanched

2   cups Egg-Cream Mixture

1   lb. fettuccine, cooked

4   teaspoons parsley, chopped

Egg-Cream Mixture

2   egg yolks

2   cups of heavy cream.

Brush chicken with olive oil. Grill chicken until done, about 10-12 minutes. Set aside.

Heat Red Bell Pepper Butter, Tomato-Basil Sauce, and Olive Oil, Garlic, & Herb Sauce in large sauté pan. Add mushrooms and asparagus and continue to cook until asparagus is tender, approximately 3 minutes. Add Egg-Cream Mixture and cook until slightly thickened.

Combine sauce mixture from sauté pan with fettuccine. Toss to coat thoroughly.

To serve: Transfer fettuccine mixture to large serving platter. Pour any sauce remaining in sauté pan over the fettuccine. Arrange chicken breast on top of fettuccine. Sprinkle with chopped parsley.

Egg-Cream Mixture: Whisk together egg yolks and heavy cream.

Robert Mueller Chardonnay – Russian River

Three Cheese Pizza

1   10″ pizza shell, homemade* or store-
    purchased shell
1   tablespoon Olive Oil, Garlic & Herb
    Sauce (see page 18)
4   tablespoons Parmesan cheese, grated
4   tablespoons fresh mozzarella cheese,
    shredded
2   tablespoons Tomato Concasse (see
    page 20)
1   tablespoon basil, julienned into thin
    strips
4   tablespoons goat cheese

*Homemade Pizza Dough
(Makes six 10″ pizza shells)
⅔   cup warm water (100°)
2   tablespoons vegetable oil
1½ teaspoons salt
1   package yeast
1   tablespoon sugar
1   cup hi-gluten flour

For Herb Pizza Dough
2   tablespoons basil, finely chopped
1   tablespoon thyme
1   tablespoon chives
2   teaspoons rosemary
add to pizza dough.

Preheat oven to 400°.

Lightly brush pizza shell with Olive Oil, Garlic, & Herb Sauce. Sprinkle with Parmesan cheese and half of the mozzarella cheese. Spoon Tomato Concasse evenly over cheese. Sprinkle with basil and remaining mozzarella cheese.

Dot with goat cheese. Drizzle remaining Olive Oil, Garlic, & Herb Sauce over entire pizza.

Bake on pizza screen or stone in oven until cheese is golden and bubbly, 10 to 15 minutes. Cut into 6 pieces and serve.

Homemade Pizza Dough: Combine water, vegetable oil, salt, yeast, and sugar in large bowl. Stir until yeast is dissolved.

Add flour and mix for approximately 5 minutes or until dough is of a smooth consistency. Remove from bowl and divide into 6 even pieces. Roll into a ball and brush lightly with oil to retain moisture. Allow to rise for 30 minutes or until doubled in size.

Roll out on floured surface to 10″ rounds. Place on pizza screeen and refrigerate until ready to bake.

Grilled Herb Pizza

¼   cup shitake mushrooms, sliced thin

¼   cup oyster mushrooms, sliced thin

¼   cup portobello mushrooms,
      sliced thin

2   teaspoons olive oil
      Herb Pizza Dough (see page 141)

1   tablespoon Olive Oil, Garlic, & Herb
      Sauce (see page 18)

1   tablespoon Tomato-Basil Sauce
      (see page 18)

2   tablespoons Rustico Red Pepper* or
      Jalapeño Jack cheese, shredded

2   tablespoons Monterey Jack cheese,
      shredded

2   tablespoons Asiago cheese, shredded

¼   red pepper, roasted & julienned into
      thin slices (see page 25)

¼   yellow pepper, roasted & julienned
      into thin slices (see page 25)

1   tablespoon Tomato Concasse (see
      page 20)

1   tablespoon basil, julienned into thin
      strips

1   tablespoon oregano, julienned into
      thin strips

Rustico Red Pepper cheese is a semi-hard Italian cheese with red pepper flakes.

Preheat oven to 450°.

In small pan, sauté mushrooms in olive oil until tender, approximately 3 to 4 minutes. Set aside.

Pregrill pizza shell. Cool. Mix together Olive Oil, Garlic, & Herb Sauce and Tomato-Basil Sauce. Brush on shell.

Sprinkle Rustico, Monterey Jack, and half of the Asiago cheese evenly over the pizza shell.

Spread red & yellow roasted peppers and sautéed mushrooms on pizza shell. Sprinkle evenly with remaining Asiago cheese. Top with Tomato Concasse, basil, and oregano.

Bake on pizza screen or stone in oven for about 10 minutes or until golden. Cut into 6 pieces.

Atlas Peak Sangiovese

Homemade Pizza Dough (see page 141)
Thin Crust Pizza Sauce

⅓ cup fontina cheese, shredded

2 tablespoons carmelized red onion

½ cup Italian sausage with fennel, cooked

¼ red bell pepper, roasted (see page 25), julienned into ¼″ strips

Thin Crust Pizza Sauce

1 tablespoon Olive Oil, Garlic & Herb Sauce (see page 18)

2 tablespoons Tomato-Basil Sauce (see page 18)

Carmelized Red Onion

1½ teaspoons olive oil

½ small red onion, julienned thin

1 teaspoon sugar

½ teaspoons red wine vinegar

Preheat oven to 500°.

Brush pizza shell with Thin Crust Pizza Sauce. Sprinkle half of the fontina cheese on sauce. Layer ingredients on pizza shell in the following order: carmelized red onion, Italian sausage, and red pepper. Top with remaining cheese.

Bake on pizza screen or stone in oven for 10 to 15 minutes or until golden and bubbly. Cut in 6 pieces.

Thin Crust Pizza Sauce: Blend thoroughly in food processor.

Carmelized Red Onion: Heat oil in sauté pan until hot. Add onions and cook until golden, approximately 10 minutes. Add sugar and vinegar and cook for 2 minutes. Remove from heat and cool.

Pastas & Pizzas

Columbia Crest Syrah - Columbia Valley

Grilled Chicken Pizza

Homemade Pizza Dough (see page 141)
Basil Pesto (see page 21)

¼	cup Romano cheese, shredded
1	piece skinless chicken breast (approximately 4 oz.), grilled, sliced very thin
¼	red pepper, roasted & julienned into thin slices
¼	yellow pepper, roasted & julienned into thin slices
¼	cup fresh mozzarella, sliced
1	tablespoon pine nuts, toasted
2	sun dried tomatoes, julienned into thin slices

Preheat oven to 400°.

Brush pizza shell with Basil Pesto. Sprinkle with 2 tablespoons of Romano cheese. Top with grilled chicken. Add roasted peppers, mozzarella, and remaining Romano cheese. Sprinkle with toasted pine nuts and sun dried tomatoes.

Bake on pizza screen or stone in oven for 10 to 15 minutes or until golden. Cut into 6 pieces.

Silverado Sauvignon Blanc - Napa

Seafood

WHEN USING SEAFOOD IT IS VERY IMPORTANT TO BUY THE FRESH-
EST AVAILABLE AND MAKE SURE YOU HAVE CONFIDENCE IN YOUR
MARKET WHEN SHOPPING. I'VE INCLUDED THE SEA BASS RECIPE
THAT I USED AS A COURSE WHEN I COOKED AT THE JAMES BEARD
HOUSE IN NEW YORK. I THINK IT IS A GREAT DISH. IT IS ALSO THE
DISH THAT APPEARS ON THE COVER OF THIS BOOK.

Hazelnut & Mustard Seed Crusted Black Grouper
with Spiced Rum Butter Sauce

6   6 oz. pieces black grouper
1   cup milk
    Hazelnut & Mustard Seed Crust
      Mixture
1   cup olive oil
⅔   cup Captain Morgan Spiced Rum®
1½ cups butter, melted
6   tablespoons hazelnuts, toasted &
      chopped
18 pieces Yukon Gold potatoes, cut into
      ½″ pieces & roasted
2   zucchini, sliced ¼″ thick on the bias
      & roasted
2   yellow squash, sliced ¼″ thick on the
      bias & roasted
18 asparagus spears, trimmed & roasted
6   teaspoons chives, chopped

Hazelnut & Mustard Seed Crust Mixture
½   cup hazelnuts, toasted & chopped
2   tablespoons mustard seed
½   cup Fry Krisp® batter mix

Remove skin from grouper. Soak fish in milk for 1 hour. Remove from milk and dust in Hazelnut & Mustard Seed Crust Mixture.

Heat oil in sauté pan. Add grouper and sauté until golden on both sides, approximately 8 to 10 minutes. Remove fish from pan and keep warm until ready to serve.

Add spiced rum to sauté pan and bring to a low boil to remove any fish from the bottom of the pan. Immediately add butter and toasted hazelnuts; mix well. Keep warm.

Arrange potatoes, zucchini, yellow squash, and asparagus on each plate. Place one piece of grouper on top of vegetables and drizzle with warm butter sauce from sauté pan. Garnish with chopped chives.

Hazelnut & Mustard Seed Crust Mixture: Combine hazelnuts, mustard seed, and Fry Krisp® batter mix. Mix together in food processor and process until well blended. Set aside.

Seafood

147

Kenwood Sauvignon Blanc - Sonoma

see photo | SERVES **4**

4   6 oz. pieces sea bass

12   littleneck clams, cleaned

3   cups New Bedford Sauce

2   cups White Cheddar Mashers (see
     page 164)

8   pieces green asparagus, trimmed

8   pieces white asparagus, trimmed

New Bedford Sauce

1   cup Garlic Butter, melted (see page 19)

1   cup white wine

1   cup Tomato-Basil Sauce (see page 18)

¼   cup small red onion, sliced thin

½   lb. pancetta, julienned fine, rendered
     crisp

2   teaspoons jalapeño pepper, seeded,
     finely chopped

Preheat grill or broiler.

Cook sea bass on each side for approximately 5 minutes. Set aside; keep warm.

In a sauté pan, steam clams with asparagus in New Bedford Sauce on medium heat until clams open, approximately 6 minutes. Remove from heat.

Place White Cheddar Mashers in the center of serving plates. Lay a piece of grilled sea bass on mashers and ladle with New Bedford Sauce. Arrange 3 clams around mashers and evenly distribute green and white asparagus.

New Bedford Sauce: Combine all ingredients thoroughly.

Sonoma Cutrer Chardonnay – Cutrer Vineyards

Maryland Crab Cakes

SERVES 6

2	lbs. jumbo lump blue crabmeat
⅓	cup dry bread crumbs
1	cup mayonnaise
2	eggs
2	tablespoons parsley, finely chopped
1	tablespoon Worcestershire sauce
2	teaspoons mustard
2	teaspoons salt
½	teaspoon white pepper
1	tablespoon red pepper, roasted & finely chopped (see page 25)
2	tablespoons butter, melted
1	teaspoon paprika
6	tablespoons Citrus Aioli (see page 29)

Carefully remove shells from crabmeat; using caution not to break the meat.

Combine crabmeat and bread crumbs in a bowl and gently blend together.

In a separate bowl combine mayonnaise, eggs, parsley, Worcestershire, mustard, salt, white pepper, and red pepper. Using a rubber spatula, gently fold into crabmeat mixture.

Refrigerate for one hour.

Preheat broiler.

Form into 12 crab cakes using ½ cup for each crab cake. Place on ovenproof tray; brush with butter and sprinkle with a little paprika. Broil until golden brown, approximately 5 to 7 minutes.

Serve with Citrus Aioli.

Seafood

149

Robert Mondavi Fume Blanc – Napa

Salmon with Arugula, Polenta, & Bacon-Balsamic Vinaigrette

4   6 oz. pieces salmon
¼   lb. wild mushrooms, morels,
        chanterelles, or porcini, sautéed
16   red teardrop tomatoes, halved
16   yellow teardrop tomatoes, halved
2   cups arugula, cleaned & trimmed
        Bacon-Balsamic Vinaigrette
12   2x2″ pieces Red Pepper Polenta

Bacon-Balsamic Vinaigrette

6   oz. bacon, diced into ½″ pieces
½   cup olive oil
2   tablespoons shallots, finely chopped
1   tablespoon garlic, finely chopped
1   tablespoon brown sugar
⅓   cup balsamic vinegar

Red Pepper Polenta

1½   cups water
4   cups vegetable stock
1   tablespoon garlic, minced
⅔   cup yellow cornmeal
⅔   cup grits
1   small red pepper, roasted & puréed
        (see page 25)
1   cup sour cream
¼   cup Monterey Jack cheese, shredded
¼   cup Parmesan cheese, grated
4   tablespoons butter
1   teaspoon salt
¼   teaspoon white pepper

Preheat broiler or grill.

Grill or broil salmon until thoroughly cooked, approximately 10 minutes. Set aside and keep warm.

Preheat oven to 350°.

In an ovenproof pan, add mushrooms, tomatoes, and arugula; toss with Bacon-Balsamic Vinaigrette. Place in oven for 5 minutes to get warm.

Place a piece of salmon on each serving plate. Arrange Red Pepper Polenta around salmon. Top with warm vegetables and vinaigrette.

Bacon-Balsamic Vinaigrette: Sauté bacon until crisp. Remove bacon, drain on paper towel and set aside. Reserve 2 oz. bacon drippings.

In clean sauté pan, combine bacon drippings and olive oil; heat.

Add shallots, garlic, and brown sugar and cook until soft. Stir in balsamic vinegar.

Add bacon and mix thoroughly.

Refrigerate until ready to serve.

Red Pepper Polenta: Preheat oven to 350°.

In an ovenproof pan, bring water, vegetable stock, and garlic to a boil. Stir in cornmeal, grits, and red pepper; reduce heat and continue cooking for 5 minutes, stirring constantly.

Cover and place in oven for 30 minutes.

Remove from oven. Stir in sour cream, cheeses, butter, salt, and white pepper; mix thoroughly. Spread on a cookie sheet and cool. Cut into 12 2x2″ squares.

Gary Farrell Pinot Noir – Russian River Valley

Grilled Asian BBQ Tuna

4   6 oz. pieces yellowfin tuna
     Honey Soy Marinade
     Asian BBQ Honey Vinaigrette
     Chef's Angel Hair Pasta
4   tablespoons pickled ginger
4   teaspoons black sesame seeds

Honey Soy Marinade

⅔   cup teriyaki sauce
3   tablespoons honey
1½   tablespoons lime juice
1   tablespoon chipotle pepper purée

Asian BBQ Honey Vinaigrette

½   cup teriyaki sauce
¼   cup honey
¼   cup rice wine vinegar
¼   cup sesame oil
1   tablespoon ginger, grated
1   green onion, thinly sliced
1   clove garlic, minced
1   teaspoon Chinese chili paste

Chef's Angel Hair Pasta

8   oz. angel hair pasta, cooked
2   tablespoons olive oil
16   pea pods, julienned
½   red pepper, julienned
½   yellow pepper, julienned
¼   cup shitake mushrooms, sliced thin
½   cup napa cabbage, sliced thin
¼   cup daikon radish, julienned
¼   cup green onions, sliced on bias

Marinate tuna in Honey Soy Marinade for 3 hours.

Prepare Asian BBQ Honey Vinaigrette. Set aside.

Prepare Chef's Angel Hair Pasta. Set aside.

Preheat grill or broiler.

Grill tuna until medium rare, or desired doneness, approximately 10 minutes. Remove tuna from grill and keep warm.

In a large sauté pan, add Asian BBQ Honey Vinaigrette and Chef's Angel Hair Pasta; toss to coat well and heat thoroughly.

Transfer pasta to a large serving platter. Place tuna on top of pasta. Garnish with pickled ginger and black sesame seeds.

Honey Soy Marinade: Combine all ingredients in mixing bowl.

Asian BBQ Honey Vinaigrette: Put all ingredients in blender and process until well blended.

Refrigerate until ready to use.

Chef's Angel Hair Pasta: Cook Angel Hair Pasta in hot water until al dente and allow to cool. In mixing bowl, toss pasta with all remaining ingredients and mix well.

Ridge Geyserville Zinfandel

Sautéed Walleye with Citrus Butter

4   6 oz. pieces walleye, skinned & cut
     in half
1   cup milk
     salt to taste
     Black Walnut Batter Mix, for dusting
1   cup vegetable oil
     Citrus Butter
1   teaspoon parsley, chopped for garnish

Black Walnut Batter Mix
½   cup cracker meal
½   cup Fry Krisp® batter mix
½   cup black walnuts, finely chopped

Citrus Butter
2   cloves garlic
½   cup butter, melted
⅓   cup orange juice
¼   cup lemon juice
2   tablespoons soy sauce
2   teaspoons lemon zest
2   teaspoons orange zest

Rinse walleye and soak in milk for 1 hour.

Season fish with salt and dust in Black Walnut Batter Mix. Heat oil in large sauté pan. Place fish in pan and cook until golden, approximately 5-6 minutes. Remove from pan.

Serve with warm Citrus Butter. Garnish with chopped parsley.

Black Walnut Batter Mix: Mix all ingredients together.

Citrus Butter: Place garlic and butter in blender and process until well blended. Transfer to bowl. Whisk in remaining ingredients.

Alexander Valley Vineyards Chardonnay | *A signature dish at The Common Grill. You can also prepare it with lake perch.*

Salmon Cakes with Warm Watercress-Red Onion Salad and Sesame Ginger Vinaigrette

1	lb. salmon
1	cup water
1	cup white wine
4	tablespoons dry bread crumbs
¼	cup mayonnaise
1	egg
2	teaspoons parsley, finely chopped
2	teaspoons Worcestershire sauce
1	teaspoon mustard
1	teaspoon salt
¼	teaspoon white pepper
1	tablespoon pimento, finely chopped
2	tablespoons butter, melted
1	teaspoon paprika
3	teaspoons chives, chopped for garnish

Watercress-Red Onion Salad

½	cup red onion, sliced ½″, grilled
2	bunches watercress, cleaned
½	cup Sesame Ginger Vinaigrette

Sesame Ginger Vinaigrette

3	tablespoons sesame oil
1½	teaspoons sugar
3	tablespoons soy sauce
1½	tablespoons fresh ginger, grated
3	tablespoons rice wine vinegar
3	tablespoons red wine vinegar
⅓	cup olive oil
½	teaspoon salt
⅛	teaspoon white pepper

Poach salmon in water and white wine until cooked, approximately 10 to 12 minutes. Remove bones from salmon. Chill.

In a large bowl, gently blend salmon with bread crumbs.

In a separate bowl, combine mayonnaise, egg, parsley, Worcestershire, mustard, salt, pepper, and pimento. Pour this mixture over salmon and bread crumbs. Carefully fold together with a spatula. Refrigerate for 1 hour.

Preheat broiler.

Form salmon mixture into 8 cakes. Place on ovenproof tray; brush with melted butter and sprinkle with paprika. Broil until golden, approximately 6 minutes. Place Salmon Cakes on a serving plate and top with equal portions of Watercress-Red Onion Salad. Top with chopped chives.

Watercress-Red Onion Salad: Brush red onion slices with olive oil and place on grill, cook both sides until soft. Cool then quarter the grilled onions. Toss onions with watercress and vinaigrette and keep warm until ready to serve with Salmon Cakes.

Sesame Ginger Vinaigrette: Combine all ingredients in a mixing bowl and mix well. Keep at room temperature.

Seafood

155

Robert Mondavi Carneros Chardonnay

Sautéed Whitefish with Michigan Bean Compote

see photo SERVES

4   6 oz. pieces whitefish, skinned
½   cup cornmeal
½   cup flour
1   cup vegetable oil
    Citrus Butter
4   teaspoons fresh chives, chopped for
      garnish
    Michigan Bean Compote

Citrus Butter
2   cloves garlic
½   cup butter, melted
⅓   cup orange juice
¼   cup lemon juice
2   tablespoons soy sauce
2   teaspoons lemon zest
2   teaspoons orange zest

Michigan Bean Compote
1   cup Northern beans
2   tablespoons olive oil
2   tablespoons red onion, finely chopped
1   tablespoon green onion, sliced on bias
¼   red pepper, diced fine
¼   yellow pepper, diced fine
¼   green pepper, diced fine
1   jalapeño pepper, finely chopped
2   cloves garlic, minced
1   teaspoon fresh rosemary, finely
      chopped
2   tablespoons parsley, finely chopped
½   teaspoon salt
    pinch white pepper
1   plum tomato, seeded & chopped
1   tablespoon lemon juice
2   teaspoons sherry wine vinegar

Mix together cornmeal and flour; dust whitefish.

Heat vegetable oil in sauté pan. Place whitefish in pan and sauté until golden, approximately 4 to 5 minutes per side. Transfer to serving plates; drizzle with Citrus Butter and sprinkle with chives. Serve with Michigan Bean Compote.

Citrus Butter: Place garlic and butter in blender and process until well blended. Transfer to bowl. Whisk in remaining ingredients.

Michigan Bean Compote: Soak beans overnight in water. Drain.

In a saucepan, bring water to a boil. Reduce heat to a simmer and cook beans for 30 minutes. Drain. Set aside.

Heat olive oil in a sauté pan. Stir in onions and cook until soft, approximately 3 to 4 minutes. Add red, yellow, and green peppers and cook until soft, approximately 5 minutes.

Stir in jalapeño, garlic, rosemary, parsley, salt, and white pepper and cook for 1 minute.

Add beans, tomato, lemon juice, and sherry wine vinegar; cook for 5 minutes. Remove from heat.

Refrigerate until ready to serve.

Good Harbor Fishtown White - Michigan

Rainbow Trout with Red Onion Marmalade

SERVES 4

4   10 oz. pieces rainbow trout
     all-purpose flour, for dusting
1   cup vegetable oil
     salt to taste
     Red Onion Marmalade
8   redskin potatoes, roasted
4   teaspoons parsley, chopped fine

Red Onion Marmalade

½   lb. red onions, julienned
2   tablespoons vegetable oil
3   tablespoons red wine vinegar
4   tablespoons sugar
2   teaspoons ketchup
     pinch cayenne pepper
     pinch white pepper

Dust trout with flour. Heat vegetable oil in large sauté pan until hot. Place trout in sauté pan, flesh side down. Sauté for 3-4 minutes on each side until golden.

Remove from pan. Top trout with Red Onion Marmalade and serve with roasted redskin potatoes. Garnish with chopped parsley.

Red Onion Marmalade: Bring a pot of water to a boil. Immerse onion in boiling water for 15 to 20 seconds. Remove from water and set aside.

Heat vegetable oil in large sauté pan. Add red onion and cook until golden, approximately 15 to 20 minutes. Stir in vinegar, sugar, ketchup, cayenne pepper, and white pepper. Continue cooking until thickened slightly, approximately 5 minutes. Remove from heat. Keep warm until ready to serve.

Seafood

158

La Crema Chardonnay - Sonoma

Pan-Seared Whitefish with Cajun Ragout Sauce

4   6 oz. pieces whitefish, skinned
4   tablespoons butter, melted
4   teaspoons Cajun seasonings
1   tablespoon olive oil
    Cajun Ragout Sauce
4   teaspoons chives, chopped

Cajun Ragout Sauce
2   tablespoons olive oil
¼   lb. Tasso ham (see page 202) or
    smoked ham
1   ear fresh corn, kernels removed from
    husk
½   small red onion, finely diced
1   clove garlic, minced
¼   teaspoon salt
    pinch black pepper
¼   lb. crawfish or shrimp tails
¼   red pepper, finely diced
1   green onion, sliced thin
¾   cup heavy cream

Brush whitefish with melted butter and season lightly with Cajun spices.

Heat olive oil in sauté pan. Add fish to pan and pan sear for approximately 6 to 8 minutes, turning after 4 minutes.

Place fish on serving plates and ladle with Cajun Ragout Sauce. Garnish with chopped chives.

Cajun Ragout Sauce: In a large sauté pan, heat olive oil. Add ham and cook for 5 minutes, or until ham is crispy. Add corn and cook for 2 to 3 minutes. Add red onion and cook for 5 minutes. Stir in garlic, salt, black pepper, crawfish tails, red pepper, and green onion; continue cooking for 3 to 4 minutes.

Blend in cream and cook over high heat for 5 minutes or until sauce is reduced by one-quarter. Remove from heat and keep warm.

Chateau St. Jean Fume Blanc – Sonoma

Pan-Seared Halibut Stew with Lobster Saffron Broth

see photo | SERVES **4**

4   6 oz. pieces halibut
1   teaspoon Cajun seasoning
¼   cup olive oil
¼   cup shitake mushrooms, sliced thin
4   plum tomatoes, seeded & diced into
        1″ pieces
1   yellow pepper, roasted & chopped
        into ½″ pieces
4   tablespoons fresh basil, julienned
4   tablespoons green onion, sliced thin
    Lobster Saffron Broth
    fresh chives, chopped for garnish
½   cup cannellini beans, precooked
¼   cup green beans
¼   cup yellow wax beans
¼   cup asparagus

Lobster Saffron Broth

2   cups water
2   cups lobster stock
1   tablespoon saffron
1   tablespoon kosher salt
1   teaspoon black pepper
1   teaspoon Cajun seasoning

Season halibut lightly with Cajun seasoning. Heat olive oil in a large sauté pan; add halibut and cook for 2 minutes. Stir in mushrooms, tomatoes, pepper, basil, onion, beans, and asparagus and sauté for 2 minutes.

Pour in Saffron Broth and cook for 4 to 5 minutes.

Remove halibut from pan and place in serving bowls. Ladle Saffron Broth and vegetables over halibut. Garnish with chopped chives.

Lobster Saffron Broth: Combine all ingredients in bowl; mix well. Refrigerate until ready to use.

Belvedere Chardonnay – Russian River Valley

Vegetables & Side Dishes

THE FOLLOWING RECIPES IN THIS CHAPTER ARE SOME SIDE DISHES WE USE CURRENTLY AND OTHERS THAT HAVE BEEN DEVELOPED OVER THE YEARS TO ACCOMPANY ENTRÉES AT THE GRILL. THESE ARE JUST AS IMPORTANT AS THE MAIN ENTRÉE.

Tuscan Beans

½ lb. cannellini beans
¼ cup pancetta, diced
1 sprig rosemary
1 sprig oregano
2 cloves garlic, minced
½ cup tomatoes, diced
¼ cup white wine
1½ cups chicken broth
1 tablespoon extra virgin olive oil
1 teaspoon kosher salt
½ teaspoon black pepper

Soak beans in water overnight. Drain. Rinse. Set aside.

Heat olive oil in sauce pan. Add pancetta and sauté until crispy.

Add remaining ingredients and cover. Simmer on low heat for 25 minutes.

Preheat oven to 300˚.

Transfer to oven and bake for 2 hours. After 2 hours check to see if additional liquid is needed. If beans are dry, add a little chicken broth and continue baking for an additional hour, or until beans are soft.

These are great with any pork dish.

Potato Leek Cake Mix

1	lb. baking potatoes
¼	teaspoon salt
	pinch black pepper
1	egg, lightly beaten
¼	cup leeks, finely chopped, sautéed in butter
2	tablespoons butter

Bring water to a boil in a large stockpot. Add potatoes and boil for 15 minutes. Remove from heat and allow to rest for 10 minutes.

Drain potatoes under slowly running cool water for 10 minutes. Refrigerate for 30 minutes.

Peel cooled potatoes and shred into large bowl. Season with salt and pepper. Add beaten egg and leeks; stir gently. Shape into 4 patties.

Heat butter in skillet; sauté patties over medium heat until golden, approximately 3 to 4 minutes.

Makes 4 cakes

Roasted Wild Mushrooms

10	cloves garlic, minced
4	tablespoons olive oil
4	tablespoons balsamic vinegar
4	sprigs fresh rosemary, chopped
4	sprigs fresh thyme, chopped
1	cup shitake mushrooms, sliced
1	cup oyster mushrooms, sliced
½	cup portobello mushrooms, sliced
¼	cup crimini mushrooms, sliced
½	teaspoon seasoning salt

Preheat oven to 400°.

In medium bowl, combine garlic, olive oil, balsamic vinegar, rosemary, and thyme. Add mushrooms and toss to coat well. Sprinkle with seasoning salt. Transfer to baking sheet and roast in oven for 25 minutes.

Makes 1 lb.

White Cheddar Mashers

2	lbs. Idaho potatoes, peeled
¼	cup Olive Oil, Garlic & Herb Sauce (see page 18)
¼	lb. white cheddar cheese
2	tablespoons melted butter
2	teaspoons seasoning salt
½	teaspoon white pepper
½	cup half-and-half
¼	cup sour cream

Cook potatoes in boiling water until soft, approximately 30 minutes. Drain and transfer to large mixing bowl and slowly mash potatoes, add remaining ingredients and beat until well blended.

Makes 1 qt.

Redskin Mashers

1½	lbs. redskin potatoes, quartered
1	small carrot, shredded
2	parsnips, quartered
1	teaspoon seasoning salt
½	teaspoon white pepper
⅓	cup sour cream
1	tablespoon scallions, finely chopped
2	tablespoons half-and-half

Cook redskins, carrot and parsnips in a large pot until redskins are tender, approximately 30 minutes. Drain and transfer to a large bowl, add remaining ingredients and beat with electric mixer until well blended.

Makes 1 qt.

Sweet Potato & Parsnip Hash Browns

1½ lbs. sweet potatoes, peeled, chopped into ½″ pieces

¼   lb. parsnips, peeled, chopped into ½″ pieces

4   strips bacon, cut into ½″ pieces

⅓   cup peanut oil

¼   lb. red onion, finely chopped

1   teaspoon salt

¼   teaspoon black pepper

1   teaspoon chopped parsley

Boil sweet potatoes and parsnips until tender. Immediately submerge in ice water to stop cooking process. Set aside.

Sauté bacon until crisp. Remove from heat. Drain. Pour in peanut oil and heat. Add red onion, cook until golden, approximately 5 minutes. Gently stir in potatoes and parsnips, sauté for 5 minutes, or until golden in color. Add salt, pepper, and parsley; mix thoroughly. Remove from heat. Serve warm.

Grilled Corn & Poblano Mashers

1	lb. Idaho potatoes, peeled
1	tablespoon butter
2	tablespoons sour cream
¼	cup half-and-half
1	teaspoon seasoned salt
	pinch white pepper
1	ear corn, grilled, kernels removed from cob
½	Poblano pepper, roasted, peeled, seeded, and cut into ½″ pieces (see page 25)

Cook potatoes in boiling water until soft, approximately 25 to 30 minutes. Drain. Place in large bowl and beat with electric mixer until smooth.

Thoroughly mix in remaining ingredients.

Serve immediately.

Serves 6

Wild Rice & Vegetable Blend

⅓	cup wild rice
⅔	cup chicken stock
1	lb. rice pilaf, cooked
2	tablespoons pecans, chopped
⅓	cup carrots, cut on bias into ¼″ pieces
¼	cup zucchini, cut on bias into ¼″ pieces
¼	cup yellow squash, cut on bias into ¼″ pieces
¼	cup red pepper, julienned into ¼″ pieces
1	green onion, sliced into ¼″ pieces

Place wild rice and chicken stock in a saucepan and bring to a boil. Cook for 20 to 30 minutes, or until rice is tender. Remove from heat and stir in cooked rice pilaf.

Add pecans and lightly steamed vegetables; mix well.

Makes 2 lbs.

Wild Rice & Apple Griddle Cakes

see photo | SERVES **12**

1½ cups Uncle Ben's® Wild Rice & Pilaf
Mix

2 green onions, chopped fine

2 tablespoons pecans, chopped

2 Granny Smith apples, chopped into
¼″ pieces

3 tablespoons butter, melted

⅓ cup all-purpose flour

1½ tablespoons baking powder

1½ tablespoons brown sugar

1 cup Jiffy® corn muffin mix

4 eggs

1 cup buttermilk

2 tablespoons honey

Cook the wild rice/pilaf mixture in boiling water, partially covered, until tender, approximately 25 to 30 minutes. Drain and rinse under cold water. Set aside.

In a separate bowl, add all remaining ingredients, mixing thoroughly to avoid lumps. Add cooked rice and mix well. Refrigerate until ready to use.

Preheat oven to 300°.

Spray a sauté pan or griddle with vegetable oil; heat. Ladle 2 tablespoons batter per cake onto pan; cook until golden. Flip cake and cook until golden on the other side, approximately 2 to 3 minutes. Keep warm until you finish the batch of cakes.

One of my favorite Thanksgiving Day side dishes.

Orzo, Wild Mushrooms, & Pancetta

see photo | SERVES 6

¼ lb. pancetta, chopped fine

1 leek, cleaned & thinly sliced

½ cup shitake mushrooms, stems
   removed & sliced

½ cup crimini mushrooms, sliced

½ cup portobello mushrooms, sliced

½ cup oyster mushrooms, sliced

½ teaspoon kosher salt

1 teaspoon lemon zest

1 tablespoon thyme

¼ teaspoon black pepper

¼ cup chicken stock

1 lb. orzo pasta, cooked

Cook pancetta in sauté pan until crispy. Drain. Add leeks and sauté until soft. Remove with a slotted spoon and set aside.

Place mushrooms in sauté pan and cook until golden, approximately 5 minutes. Add salt, zest, thyme, pepper, and leek/pancetta mixture. Add chicken broth and bring to a boil. Reduce heat to low and simmer until liquid is absorbed. Stir in orzo.

Serve immediately.

Wild Mushrooms au Gratin

½ cup button mushrooms, sliced into
    ¼″ pieces
¼ cup oyster mushrooms, sliced into
    ½″ pieces
¼ cup shitake mushrooms, stems
    removed & sliced into ⅛″ pieces
¼ cup butter, melted
¼ cup Parmesan cheese, grated
½ cup Egg/Cream Mixture

Egg/Cream Mixture
1 egg yolk
1 cup heavy cream

Heat butter in sauté pan. Add mushrooms and sauté for 4 to 5 minutes, until mushrooms are tender.

Stir in Parmesan cheese and Egg/Cream Mixture. Continue cooking until sauce begins to thicken.

Remove from heat and serve immediately.

Egg/Cream Mixture: Blend together.

Makes 2 cups

Winter Root Vegetable Gratin

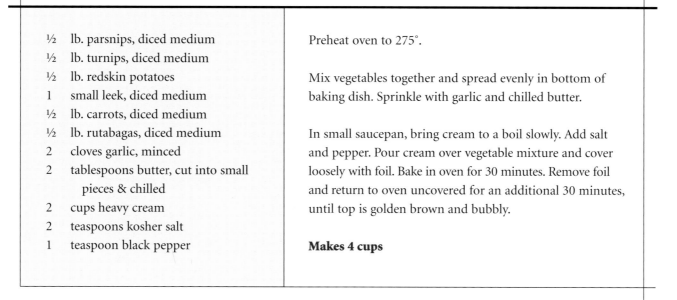

½ lb. parsnips, diced medium
½ lb. turnips, diced medium
½ lb. redskin potatoes
1 small leek, diced medium
½ lb. carrots, diced medium
½ lb. rutabagas, diced medium
2 cloves garlic, minced
2 tablespoons butter, cut into small
    pieces & chilled
2 cups heavy cream
2 teaspoons kosher salt
1 teaspoon black pepper

Preheat oven to 275°.

Mix vegetables together and spread evenly in bottom of baking dish. Sprinkle with garlic and chilled butter.

In small saucepan, bring cream to a boil slowly. Add salt and pepper. Pour cream over vegetable mixture and cover loosely with foil. Bake in oven for 30 minutes. Remove foil and return to oven uncovered for an additional 30 minutes, until top is golden brown and bubbly.

Makes 4 cups

Dried Fruit Couscous

8	oz. Moroccan couscous
1½	cups chicken broth
1	tablespoon butter
½	teaspoon salt
⅓	cup orange juice
½	teaspoon fresh ginger, grated
1	tablespoon golden raisins
3	pieces dried apricots, sliced
2	tablespoons onions, diced fine
1	tablespoon olive oil
	Ginger-Citrus Vinaigrette
1	tablespoon pimentos, finely chopped
1	tablespoon parsley, finely chopped

Ginger-Citrus Vinaigrette

2	teaspoons lemon juice
2	teaspoons orange juice
2	teaspoons ginger purée
1	clove garlic, roasted
¼	cup olive oil
1	tablespoon red onion, chopped
1	tablespoon raspberry vinegar
¼	teaspoon salt
¼	teaspoon chives, chopped

Bring chicken broth, butter, and salt to a boil. Stir in couscous, remove from heat and cover. Let stand for 6 minutes.

In separate pan, bring orange juice to a boil. Remove from heat and add ginger, raisins, apricots, and onion. Allow to steep for 5 minutes. Add to couscous and mix well.

Mix olive oil, Ginger-Citrus Vinaigrette, pimentos, and parsley into couscous. Keep warm until ready to serve.

Ginger-Citrus Vinaigrette: Place all ingredients, except chives, in a blender and purée. Transfer mixture to a bowl and add chives.

Makes 4 cups

An excellent accompaniment to roasted duck or maple cured pork.

Orzo, Radicchio, & Pancetta

¼	cup pancetta, julienned thin
1	cup orzo pasta, cooked
¼	cup Olive Oil, Garlic, & Herb sauce (see page 18)
½	cup radicchio, thinly sliced
4	pieces sun dried tomatoes, julienned
12	Calamata olives, quartered

In medium sauté pan, cook pancetta until crisp. Drain. Stir in cooked orzo and Olive Oil, Garlic, & Herb sauce; mix well.

Add remaining ingredients and toss to coat. Keep warm until ready to serve.

Serves 4

Desserts

A GREAT DINNER MENU INCLUDES A GREAT DESSERT. IT DOESN'T
HAVE TO BE FANCY, BUT IT MUST TASTE GREAT. KATE STOUGH HAS
BEEN MY PASTRY CHEF FOR SOME TIME NOW, AND SHE DOES A
GREAT JOB WORKING WITH ME ON DEVELOPING NEW THINGS. I'VE
INCLUDED MANY OF OUR GUESTS FAVORITE RECIPES IN THIS CHAP-
TER, AND I'M SURE YOU'LL BE EXCITED TO PREPARE THEM AT HOME.

Warm Berry Bread Pudding

1 cup milk
1 cup heavy cream
  pinch salt
½ teaspoon vanilla
4 eggs
½ cup sugar
6 slices egg bread, cubed
6 strawberries, sliced
36 raspberries
18 blackberries
  Cinnamon Crème Anglaise
  Raspberry Sauce
  powdered sugar, for dusting

Cinnamon Crème Anglaise

3 egg yolks
¼ cup sugar
1 cup heavy cream
⅛ teaspoon cinnamon
¼ teaspoon vanilla

Raspberry Sauce

2 pints raspberries (thawed if using
  frozen berries)
¼ cup raspberry preserves
1 tablespoon lemon juice
1 tablespoon fresh mint, julienned fine

Preheat oven to 300°.

Bring milk, cream, salt, and vanilla to a boil. As soon as mixture begins to boil, remove from heat and set aside.

In a small bowl, beat eggs and sugar until pale and thick.

Slowly add hot cream mixture to eggs, stirring to combine well. Strain into mixing bowl. Add bread cubes. Allow to rest for 30 minutes.

Arrange 1 strawberry, 6 raspberries and 3 blackberries in the bottom of each of six ramekins. Divide bread cube mixture evenly among ramekins, pouring any remaining liquid over the top of the bread pudding.

Fill an ovenproof baking pan with 2″ of water. Carefully set ramekins in baking pan and bake in oven for 45 minutes, or until golden. Remove from oven and allow to cool.

Just prior to serving reheat oven to 300°. Place ramekins in oven for 5 minutes. Remove from oven and invert on serving plate. Drizzle with Cinnamon Crème Anglaise. Spoon Raspberry Sauce around pudding. Dust with powdered sugar. Garnish with fresh mint and fresh berries.

Cinnamon Crème Anglaise: In a small bowl, whisk together egg yolks and sugar until pale in color. Set aside.

In a medium saucepan, bring cream, cinnamon, and vanilla to a boil, stirring constantly. Remove from heat.

Pour ¼ of the hot cream mixture into the egg yolk mixture; mix well. Transfer the entire yolk mixture into the saucepan containing the hot cream mixture. Cook over medium heat until sauce thickens and coats the back of a wooden spoon. Remove from heat.

Strain into clean bowl, stirring until cool.

Raspberry Sauce: Place raspberries and raspberry preserves in the bowl of a food processor, fitted with the metal blade, and purée. Strain into a bowl. Add lemon juice and mint; mix well.

Plum–Nectarine Cornmeal Crisp

1¼ lbs. fresh peaches, sliced thin
¾ lb. fresh plums, sliced thin
¾ lb. fresh nectarines, sliced thin
2 tablespoons flour
4 tablespoons sugar
1 teaspoon lemon juice
   pinch salt

Cornmeal Topping
½ cup brown sugar
1 teaspoon cinnamon
½ cup flour
½ cup yellow cornmeal
½ stick butter, softened
   vanilla ice cream for topping

Place all ingredients in bowl and combine thoroughly.

Cornmeal Topping: Combine all ingredients in bowl; mix thoroughly.

Preheat oven to 350°.

Divide the fruit mixture evenly into six 8 oz. ramekins or soufflé dishes (mixture should come to the top). Sprinkle with Cornmeal Topping.

Bake in oven for 30 minutes. Remove from oven and allow to cool.

Just prior to serving, top with a scoop of vanilla ice cream.

Strawberry-Rhubarb Crisp

1½ lbs. strawberries, sliced thick

1 lb. rhubarb, peeled, diced into ¼″ pieces,

1 tablespoon all-purpose flour

1 tablespoon sugar

2 teaspoons lemon juice

1 teaspoon cinnamon

Custard

1½ cups heavy cream

⅛ teaspoon vanilla

4 egg yolks

¼ cup sugar

Topping

2 tablespoons brown sugar

¼ cup all purpose flour

¼ cup rolled oats

¼ cup pecan pieces, toasted

pinch cinnamon

pinch kosher salt

2 tablespoons butter, softened

vanilla ice cream for topping

Place all ingredients in a bowl and combine well. Set aside.

Custard: Place cream and vanilla in a saucepan and bring to a slight boil. Set aside.

Meanwhile, in a medium size bowl beat together egg yolks and sugar until pale and slightly thick. Slowly pour in the hot cream and vanilla mixture, stirring constantly. Return to saucepan and cook until thickened. Strain. Cool.

Topping: Combine all dry ingredients in mixing bowl. Add softened butter and mix thoroughly.

Preheat oven to 350°.

Fill each of six 8 oz. ramekins ¾ from the top with the fruit mixture. Top with ¼ cup of Custard. Sprinkle with Topping.

Bake in oven for 35 to 40 minutes, until golden. Remove from oven and cool. Just prior to serving, top with a scoop of vanilla ice cream.

Desserts

This is a reminder of my Mother's Strawberry-Rhubarb Pie

2   cups heavy cream
⅛   teaspoon vanilla
5   egg yolks
⅓   cup + 1 tablespoon sugar
¼   cup bittersweet chocolate, chopped
3   croissants, toasted, cut into ½″ pieces
     Cinnamon Crème Anglaise
     Mocha Crème Anglaise
     Caramel Sauce
     fresh raspberries for garnish
     powdered sugar for dusting

Cinnamon Crème Anglaise

3   egg yolks
¼   cup sugar
1   cup heavy cream
⅛   teaspoon cinnamon
¼   teaspoon vanilla

Mocha Crème Anglaise

2   egg yolks
¼   cup sugar
¼   teaspoon espresso beans, ground
½   cup heavy cream
½   cup half-and-half
2   tablespoons chocolate, chopped
¼   teaspoon vanilla

Caramel Sauce

1½   cups sugar
⅔   cup water
1   cup heavy cream

Preheat oven to 300°.

In a small saucepan, over medium heat, bring cream and vanilla to a gentle boil. Remove from heat. Cover and allow to rest for 15 minutes.

Beat egg yolks and sugar in a small bowl until slightly thickened and pale in color. Gradually whisk cream and vanilla into sugar mixture. Return saucepan to stove and over medium heat, cook until thickened, stirring constantly. Strain.

Divide chocolate pieces into six individual 8 oz. ramekins. Fill with croissant pieces. Pour cream mixture over each. Place ramekins in water bath* and bake in oven for 1 hour, or until set. Remove from water bath and cool.

When ready to serve, reheat oven to 300°. Place ramekins in oven for 5 minutes to warm. Remove from oven and invert ramekin onto serving plate. Drizzle with a combination of Cinnamon Crème Anglaise, Mocha Crème Anglaise, and Caramel Sauce. Arrange several raspberries near pudding and dust all with powdered sugar.

Create a water bath by filling an ovenproof pan to approximately half full with water.

Cinnamon Crème Anglaise: In a small bowl, whisk together egg yolks and sugar until pale in color. Set aside.

In a medium saucepan, bring cream, cinnamon, and vanilla to a boil, stirring constantly. Remove from heat.

Pour ¼ of the hot cream mixture into the egg yolk mixture; mix well. Transfer the entire yolk mixture into the saucepan containing the hot cream mixture. Cook over medium heat until sauce thickens and coats the back of a wooden spoon. Remove from heat.

Strain into clean bowl, stir until cool.

We served this dessert at the James Beard House in New York.

Desserts

Mocha Crème Anglaise: Whisk egg yolks in a stainless steel bowl with sugar and espresso beans. Set aside. In a medium saucepan, bring the cream and half-and-half to a gentle boil. Remove from heat and whisk into egg yolk mixture. Return mixture to saucepan and continue cooking until slightly thickened. Strain. Add chopped chocolate. Allow to rest for 30 seconds, then whisk until smooth. Chill. Stir in vanilla.

Caramel Sauce: In a stainless steel saucepan, over low heat, combine sugar and water and stir until sugar is dissolved. Increase the heat slightly and continue cooking until the mixture is a golden amber color. Remove from heat and pour in all of the heavy cream. Use caution when adding the heavy cream, it will splatter.

Buttermilk-Lemon Pudding Cake

see photo | SERVES

2   cups sugar

⅔   cup all-purpose flour

1   cup lemon juice

1½   cups butter, melted

3   tablespoons lemon zest

18   egg yolks

4½   cups buttermilk

9   egg whites

⅔   cup sugar

     powdered sugar for dusting

     fresh mint for garnish

Blackberry Sauce

1   lb. blackberries

¼   cup sugar

1   tablespoon Grand Marnier® liqueur, optional

1   teaspoon lemon juice

Preheat oven to 300˚.

Thoroughly spray eight individual 8 oz. custard cups with vegetable spray.

Blend 1 cup of the sugar with the flour in a mixing bowl. Add lemon juice, butter, lemon zest, and egg yolks; mix well. Stir in buttermilk.

In separate bowl, beat egg whites until they form soft peaks. Gradually add remaining cup of sugar, while continuing to beat until stiff peaks form. Gently fold egg whites into buttermilk mixture.

Pour batter into custard cups. Place custard cups in water bath* and bake in oven for approximately 1½ hours, until top of custard is golden. Remove from water bath and cool.

To serve, invert custard cup on serving plate. Drizzle with Blackberry Sauce. Sprinkle with powdered sugar and garnish with fresh mint. Serve with fresh blackberries, if available.

Create a water bath by filling an ovenproof pan to approximately half full with water.

Blackberry Sauce: Place all ingredients in blender and purée. Strain to remove seeds. Chill until ready to serve.

Crème Brûlée with Fresh Berries

1½ cups heavy cream
4   tablespoons sugar
4   egg yolks
1   teaspoon vanilla
1   tablespoon brandy, optional
½   teaspoon superfine sugar
     raspberries, blackberries, or straw-
        berries for garnish
     mint leaves, for garnish

Preheat oven to 325°.

Heat heavy cream and sugar in a saucepan over low heat. Remove from heat and cool for 15 minutes. Thoroughly whisk in egg yolks. Blend in vanilla and brandy.

Pour mixture into ceramic soufflé dishes and place in an ovenproof pan, filled halfway with water. Bake in oven for 45 minutes, or until light brown on top. Remove from oven. Cover with plastic wrap, taking care not to let the plastic wrap touch the custard. Cool.

Preheat broiler.

Sprinkle top of each Crème Brûlée with sugar and place under broiler until carmelized.*

Serve with berries and mint leaves.

At the restaurant we use a small butane torch. Most kitchen stores also sell a mini butane torch that works perfectly.

Kahlua–Macadamia Nut Crème Brûlée

1½ cups heavy cream

¼ cup sugar

4 egg yolks

½ teaspoon vanilla

1 tablespoon Kahlua liqueur

6 teaspoons macadamia nuts, chopped
& toasted

6 teaspoons coconut, toasted

6 teaspoons superfine sugar, for garnish
Chocolate Sauce

Chocolate Sauce

3 oz. bar semisweet chocolate, chopped

3 oz. bar bittersweet chocolate, chopped

1 cup heavy cream

3 tablespoons light corn syrup

1 tablespoon butter, softened

Preheat oven to 325°.

In a medium saucepan, combine cream and sugar and cook over low heat. Remove from heat and cool for 15 minutes. Whisk in egg yolks. Blend in vanilla and Kahlua.

Sprinkle ½ teaspoon toasted macadamia nuts and ½ teaspoon toasted coconut in bottom of each soufflé dish. Pour custard into soufflé dishes and place in an ovenproof pan filled halfway with water. Bake in oven for 45 minutes or until custard begins to firm. Remove from oven and cool.

Preheat broiler.

Sprinkle top of each brulee with superfine sugar and place under broiler until carmelized.*

Sprinkle with toasted coconut and toasted macadamia nuts. Drizzle with Chocolate Sauce.

Chocolate Sauce: Place chocolate in a medium bowl and set aside.

In a medium saucepan, bring cream and corn syrup to a boil. Slowly pour over chocolate, while stirring with a rubber spatula, until chocolate is melted. Add butter; blend thoroughly.

*At the restaurant we use a small butane torch. Most kitchen stores also sell a mini butane torch that works perfectly.

Berry Shortcake with White Chocolate Cream

see photo | SERVES **4**

8   shortcake biscuits
    White Chocolate Cream
4   strawberries, sliced thin
20 raspberries
4   tablespoons Raspberry Sauce
4   tablespoons Blackberry Sauce
1   cup assorted berries
    powdered sugar, for dusting

Shortcake Biscuits

½   cup all-purpose flour
1   tablespoon sugar
1   teaspoon baking powder
1½ tablespoons butter, cut in pieces &
       chilled
2   tablespoons + 1 teaspoon heavy cream
1   hard-boiled egg yolk, mashed
1½ teaspoons butter, melted

White Chocolate Cream

6   oz. white chocolate, chopped
4   tablespoons milk
1   cup whipped cream
½   teaspoon vanilla

Raspberry Sauce

2   pints raspberries (thawed, if frozen)
¼   cup raspberry preserves
1   tablespoon lemon juice
1   tablespoon fresh mint, julienned fine

Blackberry Sauce

½   lb. blackberries
2   tablespoons sugar
1½ teaspoons Grand Marnier® liqueur,
       optional
    squeeze lemon juice

Prepare biscuits. Set aside.

Prepare White Chocolate Cream. Keep cold until ready to serve.

Place a shortcake biscuit on each of four serving plates. Place ¼ cup White Chocolate Cream on top of biscuit. Place sliced strawberry in a pinwheel on cream. Top with a second biscuit. Spoon White Chocolate Cream on biscuit. Arrange 5 raspberries on top.

Spoon fresh assorted berries around biscuits on plate. Drizzle with Raspberry and Blackberry sauces and sprinkle with powdered sugar.

Shortcake Biscuits: Preheat oven to 300˚.

Sift flour, sugar, and baking powder into a bowl. Add chilled butter pieces and mix until butter is blended into flour. Mixture will be the consistency of sand.

Add cream and egg yolk; mix well. Dough will hold together.

Turn dough onto floured work surface. Knead lightly until smooth. Roll dough out to ½″ thickness. Cut into 8 rounds with biscuit cutter. Place on greased cookie sheet. Brush with melted butter and sprinkle with sugar.

Bake in oven until golden, approximately 8 to 10 minutes. Remove from oven and store at room temperature.

White Chocolate Cream: Melt chocolate over a double boiler until smooth. Remove from heat.

In a separate pan, bring milk to a simmer. Whisk into chocolate mixture. Cool.

Gently fold in whipped cream and vanilla. Refrigerate until ready to serve.

Raspberry Sauce: Place raspberries and raspberry preserves in the bowl of a food processor, fitted with the metal blade, and purée. Strain into a bowl. Add lemon juice and mint; mix well.

Blackberry Sauce: Place all ingredients in blender and purée. Strain to remove seeds. Chill until ready to serve.

Apple & Cherry Cobbler

⅓ cup butter, melted
½ cup brown sugar
1½ tablespoons cinnamon
3 lbs. apples such as Granny Smith or
    Jonathan, sliced
1 lb. tart cherries
¼ cup golden raisins
2 tablespoons walnuts, chopped

Cobbler Topping
½ cup butter, softened
¼ cup brown sugar
½ cup sugar
¾ teaspoon cinnamon
1 cup flour
    vanilla ice cream for topping

Preheat oven to 300°.

Combine melted butter, brown sugar, and cinnamon in a large mixing bowl. Add apples, cherries, raisins, and walnuts; mix well.

Divide evenly among eight individual 8 oz. ramekins or an 8x8″ baking dish.

Top evenly with Cobbler Topping. Bake in oven for 1 hour or until topping is brown and crisp. Remove from oven and cool. Serve warm with scoop of vanilla ice cream.

Cobbler Topping: Place butter, brown sugar, sugar, and cinnamon in a bowl and combine thoroughly. Add flour and stir until flour is just blended. Set aside until ready to use.

Peach, Blueberry & Blackberry Cobbler

2   cups peaches, cut into ½″ slices
1   cup blueberries
1   cup blackberries
1   tablespoon flour
1   teaspoon cinnamon
1   tablespoon sugar
½   teaspoon lemon juice
     pinch of salt

Streusel Topping
2   tablespoons butter, softened
2   tablespoons brown sugar
     pinch of cinnamon
¼   cup flour
¼   cup rolled oats
2   tablespoons pecans, toasted

Preheat oven to 350°.

In large bowl, combine all ingredients. Divide evenly among six 8 oz. ovenproof baking dishes and sprinkle with Streusel Topping.

Bake in oven for 30 minutes or until topping is golden.

Best served warm, topped with your favorite ice cream.

Streusel Topping: Place all ingredients in the bowl of a food processor, fitted with the metal blade, and pulsate until the butter is thoroughly combined and the mixture is the size of peas.

Peanut Butter Pie

½ cup butter, melted
1 20 oz. package Nabisco® chocolate
    wafer cookies, crushed
20 oz. cream cheese, softened
1 cup sugar
20 oz. creamy peanut butter
2 cups heavy cream
1 cup powdered sugar
1½ cups honey roasted peanuts, chopped
    hot fudge sauce

Combine melted butter and cookie crumbs in a bowl; mix well. Press into a 9″ springform pan, covering 2″ on the sides. Set aside.

Combine cream cheese and sugar in bowl. Beat with electric mixer until smooth. Add peanut butter and continue beating until peanut butter is blended. Set aside.

In separate bowl, beat heavy cream and powdered sugar until stiff peaks form. Gently fold one-third into peanut butter mixture. Repeat, adding one-third of the whipped cream at a time.

Pour into prepared springform pan. Sprinkle with honey roasted peanuts.

Freeze until firm.

Remove from pan and serve with your favorite hot fudge sauce.

Refrigerate leftovers.

Chocolate Fudge Cake

12 oz. semisweet chocolate, chopped

8 oz. butter

6 eggs, separated

⅔ cup sugar

⅔ cup all-purpose flour
powdered sugar for dusting

Sugar Pecans

1 cup pecan halves

¼ cup butter, melted

2 tablespoons sugar

Chocolate Sauce

3 oz. bar semisweet chocolate, chopped

3 oz. bar bittersweet chocolate, chopped

1 cup heavy cream

3 tablespoons light corn syrup

1 tablespoon butter, softened

Preheat oven to 300°.

In a double boiler, melt chocolate and butter. Set aside to cool.

In a separate bowl, beat egg yolks until light. Slowly add the sugar, continuing to beat until mixture is a pale yellow.

Transfer melted chocolate to a large bowl and fold in yolk mixture. Add flour, stirring until thoroughly mixed.

In a separate bowl, whisk egg whites until soft peaks form. Fold one-half of egg whites into flour mixture. Repeat with remaining egg whites.

Pour into greased 9″ springform pan; tap to set. Bake in oven for 90 minutes. Remove from oven and cool.

Sprinkle cake with 1 tablespoon Sugar Pecans and drizzle with Chocolate Sauce. Dust lightly with powdered sugar.

Sugar Pecans: Preheat oven to 350°.

Toss pecan halves with butter and sugar. Spread on a cookie sheet and bake in oven for 10 minutes. Cool. Store in an airtight container.

Chocolate Sauce: Place chocolate in a medium bowl and set aside.

In a medium saucepan, bring heavy cream and corn syrup to a boil. Slowly pour over chocolate, stirring with a rubber spatula until chocolate is melted. Add butter, stirring until thoroughly mixed.

Chocolate Truffle Tart

see photo | MAKES ONE 9″ TART

1	cup pecans, toasted & coarsely ground
1	cup graham cracker crumbs
4	tablespoons butter, melted
2	tablespoons sugar
1	lb. semisweet chocolate, chopped
1	cup heavy cream
6	eggs, beaten
⅔	cup sugar
⅓	cup flour
	Crème Anglaise
	Caramel Sauce
	powdered sugar for dusting

Crème Anglaise

3	egg yolks
¼	cup sugar
1	cup heavy cream
¼	teaspoon vanilla

Caramel Sauce

1½	cups sugar
⅔	cup water
1	cup heavy cream

Preheat oven to 300°.

Place pecans, graham cracker crumbs, melted butter, and sugar in bowl; mix thoroughly. Press into the bottom and 1½″ up the sides of a 9″ springform pan. Set aside.

In a saucepan, slowly heat chocolate and cream, until chocolate is melted. Transfer to bowl. Set aside.

In a separate large bowl, combine eggs and sugar; beat until thick and pale in color. Fold in flour and mix well. Fold in melted chocolate. Pour into prepared springform pan.

Bake in oven for 45 minutes. Cool. Serve with Crème Anglaise and Caramel Sauce. Dust with powdered sugar.

Crème Anglaise: In a small bowl, whisk together egg yolks and sugar until pale in color. Set aside.

In a medium saucepan, bring cream and vanilla to a boil, stirring constantly. Remove from heat.

Pour one-fourth of the hot cream mixture into the egg yolk mixture; mix well. Transfer the entire yolk mixture into the saucepan containing the hot cream mixture. Cook over medium heat until sauce thickens and coats the back of a wooden spoon. Remove from heat.

Strain into clean bowl; stir until cool.

Caramel Sauce: In a stainless steel saucepan, over low heat, combine sugar and water and stir until sugar is dissolved. Increase the heat slightly and continue cooking until the mixture is a golden amber color. Remove from heat and pour in all of the heavy cream. Use caution when adding the heavy cream, it will splatter.

Key Lime Pie

2 teaspoons unflavored gelatin

1 cup key lime juice

6 eggs

2¼ cups sugar

2 teaspoons lime zest

⅔ cup butter, melted
Whipped Cream

10 teaspoons coconut, toasted, for garnish

10 teaspoons lime zest

Whipped Cream

1 cup heavy cream

2 tablespoons powdered sugar

Gingersnap Crust

1½ cups gingersnap cookies, finely
ground

1½ cups graham cracker crumbs

½ cup macadamia nuts, finely ground

½ cup melted butter

Gingersnap Crust: Combine ingredients in mixing bowl and mix well. Press crumbs into bottom of a 9″ springform pan and 2″ high along sides. Bake in 300° oven for 5 minutes. Allow to cool.

Place gelatin and ¼ cup of key lime juice in a bowl and allow to stand for 5 minutes.

In a medium bowl, whisk eggs and sugar until smooth and pale. Stir in gelatin/lime juice mixture, remaining lime juice and lime zest. Using a double boiler, cook until mixture is thick. Remove from heat and immediately stir in butter.

Pour into prebaked pie shell. Cool overnight in refrigerator. This must set for 24 hours before cutting.

Top with whipped cream, toasted coconut, and lime zest.

Whipped Cream: Whip cream until stiff. Thoroughly mix in sugar.

White Chocolate Cheesecake

1	20 oz. package chocolate wafers (Nabisco®)
½	cup butter, melted
½	lb. cream cheese
⅔	cup sugar
4	eggs
2	teaspoons vanilla
6	ozs. white chocolate, melted
	Raspberry Sauce
	fresh berries for garnish

Raspberry Sauce

2	pints raspberries (thawed, if frozen)
¼	cup raspberry preserves
1	tablespoon lemon juice
1	tablespoon fresh mint, julienned fine

Preheat oven to 350°.

To make the crust: grind chocolate wafers until very fine. Stir in melted butter and mix thoroughly. Press into the bottom of a 9″ springform pan and 2″ up the sides. Set aside.

Beat cream cheese with electric mixer until smooth. Slowly add sugar and continue beating until batter is smooth and there are no lumps. Add eggs, one at a time, followed by the vanilla. Thoroughly mix in white chocolate. Pour batter into prepared springform pan.

Place pan in an ovenproof baking dish filled with 2″ of water. Bake in oven for 55 to 60 minutes.

Drizzle with Raspberry Sauce and top with fresh berries.

Raspberry Sauce: Place raspberries and raspberry preserves in the bowl of a food processor, fitted with the metal blade, and purée. Strain into a bowl. Add lemon juice and mint; mix well.

Cream Puffs

see photo | MAKES **10**

2   eggs
⅓   cup water
3   tablespoons butter, cut into ½″ cubes
     pinch salt
⅓   cup all-purpose flour, sifted
1½   tablespoons sliced almonds
     coffee ice cream
     Bittersweet Chocolate Sauce
     Candied Almonds
     powdered sugar, for dusting
1   egg, beaten

Bittersweet Chocolate Sauce

1   cup cocoa powder
½   cup sugar
1¼   cups water
½   cup cream
4   tablespoons bittersweet chocolate
2   tablespoons butter

Candied Almonds

¼   cup sugar
2   tablespoons water
½   cup slivered almonds, toasted

Preheat oven to 425°.

In a small bowl, beat eggs. Set aside.

Combine water, butter, and salt in a saucepan. Heat until butter is melted. Increase heat and bring to a boil; immediately remove from heat.

Using a wire whisk, blend in flour until mixture pulls away from the sides of the pan. Return to heat and stirring constantly cook for 45 seconds, or until mixture forms a smooth ball.

Add eggs and beat until mixture forms a smooth, soft dough. Cool.

Line a cookie sheet with parchment paper and spray with vegetable spray.

Using a tablespoon, divide batter into 10 portions and place on cookie sheet. Brush with beaten egg. Sprinkle with sliced almonds.

Bake in oven for 15 minutes. Reduce heat to 250° and continue baking until puffs are golden, approximately 5 minutes. Remove from oven. Cool.

Cut tops from Cream Puffs. Fill with a scoop of coffee ice cream. Replace tops. Ladle warm Bittersweet Chocolate Sauce over Cream Puffs. Garnish with Candied Almonds and dust with powdered sugar.

Bittersweet Chocolate Sauce: Combine cocoa, sugar, and water in a saucepan. Bring to a boil and cook for 5 minutes, while whisking constantly.

Stir in the cream; return to a boil and continue cooking for 2 to 3 minutes.

Remove from heat and whisk in chocolate and butter. Return to heat and bring to a boil. Immediately remove from heat once chocolate boils. Serve warm.

Candied Almonds: In a sauté pan heat sugar and water until liquid is golden. Add almonds and toss to coat. Spread almond mixture on a cookie sheet to cool.

Break into pieces.

Macadamia Nut, White & Bittersweet Chocolate Cookies

see photo | DOZEN 2

½	cup flour
¼	teaspoon baking soda
¼	teaspoon salt
¼	cup butter, softened
¼	cup brown sugar
2	tablespoons sugar
1	egg
½	teaspoon vanilla
⅓	cup macadamia nuts, chopped
¼	cup white chocolate, chopped
¼	cup bittersweet chocolate, chopped

Preheat oven to 350°.

Sift together flour, baking soda and salt. Set aside.

Using an electric mixer, cream butter, brown sugar, and sugar; continue beating for 2 to 3 minutes until batter is fluffy and light.

Add egg and vanilla; mix well.

Stir in flour mixture.

Add nuts and both chocolates.

Drop 2 tablespoons per cookie onto cookie sheet, spaced 2″ apart. Bake in oven for approximately 10 minutes.

Peanut Butter Cookies

see photo on page 194 | DOZEN 2

1½ cups all-purpose flour
1½ tablespoons baking soda
½   teaspoon baking powder
¼   teaspoon salt
1   cup butter, softened
2   cups peanut butter
1   cup brown sugar
1   cup white sugar
2   eggs
2   tablespoons orange juice
2   teaspoons vanilla
1   cup honey roasted peanuts

Mix flour, baking soda, baking powder, and salt together in bowl. Set aside.

In a large bowl, using an electric mixer, cream together butter and peanut butter. Add brown and white sugar; continue beating on highest speed until fluffy. Beat in eggs, orange juice, and vanilla. Add flour mixture and honey roasted peanuts. Stir until combined — do not overmix.

Drop 2 tablespoons per cookie onto cookie sheet, spaced 2˝ apart, and refrigerate for 30 minutes.

Preheat oven to 300°.

Remove from refrigerator and bake in oven until golden, approximately 15 minutes.

Chocolate Fudge Cookies

1½	cups all-purpose flour
1	cup unsweetened cocoa
1	teaspoon baking soda
1	teaspoon salt
1	cup semisweet chocolate pieces
½	cup unsweetened chocolate
1⅓	cups brown sugar
⅔	cup butter
4	eggs
1	teaspoon vanilla

Preheat oven to 300°.

Sift together flour, cocoa, baking soda, and salt. Set aside.

Over medium heat, in bottom half of double boiler heat 1″ of water; do not boil.
Place semisweet chocolate pieces and unsweetened chocolate in top half of double boiler and melt slowly. Remove from heat and stir until smooth. Set aside.

Set mixer to medium speed and cream brown sugar and butter in large mixing bowl for 1 minute. Scrap sides of bowl and continue mixing while adding eggs one at a time until combined. Add vanilla and beat for 30 seconds. Add melted chocolate and beat for 10 seconds.

Slowly add sifted flour mixture to creamed mixture and continue to beat for 30 seconds. Scrap down sides with rubber spatula.

Drop 2 tablespoons per cookie onto cookie sheet, spaced 2″ apart, and bake for 15 minutes. Cool.

Oatmeal Raisin Cookies

see photo on page 197 | DOZEN **2**

1½ cups all purpose flour
1   teaspoon baking soda
1   teaspoon cinnamon
¾   cup butter, softened
½   cup brown sugar
1   cup sugar
1   egg, beaten
1   teaspoon vanilla
1½ cups rolled oats
1   cup golden raisins

Preheat oven to 275°.

Combine flour, baking soda, and cinnamon in medium size bowl. Set aside.

Cream butter with sugars until batter is fluffy. Mix in beaten egg and vanilla. Add dry ingredients a little at a time. Batter will be stiff. Stir in rolled oats and raisins. Chill dough for one hour.

Drop 2 tablespoons per cookie onto a lightly greased cookie sheet, spaced 2″ apart. Bake for 20 minutes.

Sugar Cookies

see photo on page 197 DOZEN 2

1½ cups butter, softened
2¼ cups sugar + ½ cup for rolling
3   eggs
1   tablespoon cream of tartar
4   cups flour
1½ teaspoons baking soda
¼   teaspoon salt

Place butter and sugar in bowl; cream together on medium speed with electric mixer, until light and fluffy. Add eggs and beat until mixture is smooth.

In separate bowl, combine cream of tartar, flour, baking soda, and salt. Fold into butter mixture.

Shape dough into balls (about 2 tablespoons in size) and roll lightly in sugar. Refrigerate cookie dough for 15 minutes.

Preheat oven to 300°.

Place cookies on cookie sheet 2″ apart. Bake in oven for 12 minutes or until golden.

Chocolate Chip Cookies

see photo on page 197 | DOZEN **2**

1   stick butter, softened
1   cup brown sugar
2   eggs
1   tablespoon vanilla
2½   cups all-purpose flour
1   teaspoon baking soda
1   teaspoon salt
2½   cups chocolate chips

In large mixing bowl cream the butter on medium speed until light and fluffy. Continue mixing slowly while adding the brown sugar. Batter should be light and fluffy. Add egg and vanilla. Gently fold in dry ingredients and chocolate chips.

Chill dough for 30 minutes.

Drop 2 tablespoons per cookie onto a nonstick or greased cookie sheet, spaced 2″ apart. Chill for 1 hour.

Preheat oven to 300˚.

Bake in oven for 15 minutes or until golden.

Chocolate Brownies

½ cup flour
4 tablespoons cocoa powder
2 tablespoons baking powder
½ cup butter
1¼ cups semisweet chocolate pieces
6 eggs
2 cups sugar
2 teaspoons vanilla
½ cup sour cream
1 cup walnuts

Preheat oven to 325°.

Sift together flour, cocoa, and baking powder. Set aside.

Melt butter and semisweet chocolate pieces in a double boiler. Set aside.

Place eggs, sugar, and vanilla in a mixing bowl and beat until thick. Stir in chocolate mixture. Add dry ingredients and stir until just blended. Do not overmix. Stir in sour cream and nuts.

Pour into a greased 8x10″ baking pan. Bake in oven for 1 hour. Remove from oven and allow to cool before serving.

Sources

Earthly Delights
4180 Keller Road
Suite B
Holt, MI   48842
(800) 367-4709
Specialty produce, mushrooms, & herbs

Previn Inc.
2044 Rittenhouse Square
Philadelphia, PA   19103
(212) 985-1996
Specialty cookware and bakeware

J.B. Prince
36 East 31st Street
New York, NY   10016
(212) 683-3553
Specialty cookware

Zingerman's
422 Detroit Street
Ann Arbor, MI 48104
(888) 636-8162
Specialty sausages, cheeses, Tasso ham,
Chorizo sausage, & olive oils

Balducci's Mail Order Division
95 Sherwood Ave.
Farmingdale, NY   11735
(800) 247-2450
www.balducci.com
Tasso ham, Chorizo sausage, game,
cheeses, & specialty products

The Chef's Garden
9009 Huron Avery Road
Huron, OH   44839
(800) 289-4644
Specialty produce

Smokehouse Inc.
15 Coventry Street
Roxbury, MA   02119
(617) 442-6840
Smoked chicken

Penzey's Spice House
P.O. Box 933
W 9362 Apollo Dr.
Muskego, WI   53150
(800) 741-53150
Assorted Spices

www.ethnicgrocers.com
Specialty ethnic foods
Chinese Chili Paste, Cilantro–Chili Tortillas
Hoisin sauce, Masa flour

All Serve, Inc.
PO Box 21743
Cleveland, OH   44121
(800) 827-8328
www.soupbase.com
Seafood Base

www.cooking.com
Specialty kitchenware and food

www.wine.com
Wine buying and learning

Index